Feng Shui in Singapore

FENG SHUI IN SINGAPORE

SARA NOBLE

Graham Brash
Singapore

© Sara Noble, 1994

First Published in 1994 by
Graham Brash (Pte) Ltd
32 Gul Drive
Singapore 2262

ISBN   981-218-021-4
All rights reserved

The author and publisher wish to thank Mr. Koh Kok Wah for photographs 1, 2, 7, 12 & 13 and Mr. Hamish Macdonald for illustrations 5, 8, 9, 10 & 11 featured in the book.

Cover designed by Catherine Mason
Cover illustration by Hamish Macdonald
Back cover photo by Erica Tiedemann
Typeset by Syarikat Broadway Typesetting Sdn. Bhd.
Printed in Singapore by
General Printing Services Pte. Ltd.

CONTENTS

Foreword i
Introduction iii
1. What is Feng Shui? 1
2. The Geomancers and Their Business 19
3. Using Feng Shui in the Home and Other Buildings 37
4. Landscape and Location 61
5. The Government, the Public and Feng Shui 77
6. Geomancy and Environmental Ideas 86
Appendix One: Conclusions 100
Appendix Two: List of Geomancers Interviewed 105
Glossary 106
Bibliography 108
Index 110

FOREWORD

The art of *feng shui* is one of the many valuable treasures in the Chinese culture. This art, invented by the ancient Chinese people many thousands of years ago, is an effective tool employed by the Chinese to exploit the beneficial influences existing in the environment. The subject reflects the profound wisdom of the Chinese people in understanding the abstract forces at play in the Universe and how to achieve harmony with the laws of nature.

Through the ages, this valuable art has been treated with high respect and is commonly employed as an essential guide in building Chinese palaces, residences and temples as well as selecting grave sites for burying ancestors. The astonishing validity and effectiveness of ancient arts and practices such as Chinese martial arts, herbal medicine, acupuncture, *qi gong*, *tai chi* exercise, *I Ching*, *feng shui* and the Four Pillars of Destiny are capturing global attention. Hence we are now living in an age where buried ancient wisdoms are being rediscovered for modern application and for supplementing Western technocentric sciences.

I have always felt that the valuable knowledge of *feng shui* should not be kept a secret by the Chinese masters and that its benefit should be shared by one and all. As such, I wrote *feng shui* books in English and encouraged non-Chinese intellectuals to study the subject. I am glad that Ms. Sara Noble, a non-Chinese academic from New Zealand, is not only interested in Chinese culture but has also conducted serious research into *feng shui* practices in Singapore. The result is an interesting and informative report providing an overview of the state of the business as perceived from an academic and impartial angle. As this kind of survey is sadly lacking in the field, I think that Ms. Noble's efforts are rewarding and fruitful, and the information revealed is also a good reference for practising geomancers.

Feng Shui in Singapore is exactly the kind of work which will help the subject progress in the right direction. Owing to the language barrier, cultural background and limited information sources, it is not possible to provide more detailed coverage of such a complicated and vast subject, but it is indeed an interesting book which will contribute to the understanding and progress of *feng shui*.

RAYMOND LO
Author of Feng Shui & Destiny and
Feng Shui: The Pillars of Destiny

INTRODUCTION

Feng Shui in Singapore was adapted from a thesis prepared as part of a Master of Arts degree in Geography at the University of Auckland, New Zealand. The research was conducted in 1990. To my knowledge, it is the first of its kind to be carried out in Singapore as it appears that no surveys of Singaporean geomancers have been performed before.

The aim of this study is primarily to examine the nature of *feng shui* as it is practised in Singapore. Initially it was based on the assumption that in a country where the population is more than 80% Chinese, *feng shui* would be very influential. Some of the results, however, have been a little surprising. Certainly, Singapore has a unique history and this has affected the way *feng shui* has developed. These differences are fascinating and I believe that clearly identifiable forces have produced a unique geomantic tradition.

The main areas of focus for the study are the beliefs and practices of those actively using *feng shui* in Singapore today: professional geomancers and their clients. It is not a general survey of *feng shui* practice in Singapore in that it doesn't strictly measure the extent of use of *feng shui* or its impact on the society or environment. These subjects are discussed but my approach to them is rather impressionistic and subjective. More specifically, the study is an attempt to record the types of practices and beliefs found among geomancers and their clients.

17 geomancers were approached for interviews. Only ten consented to be interviewed but this included all but two of the most prominent geomancers in Singapore. However, I am now sure that this is only a small proportion of the total number of geomancers practising at some level in Singapore. This sample represents the most professional end of the geomancy spectrum.

Much of the content of this book is descriptive and anecdotal. It includes a large number of geomantic stories from Singapore that have never been published before.

Chapter One is a fairly detailed discussion of the principles of *feng shui*, both traditional and modern. This is intended to help people understand the deeper reasoning behind *feng shui*, not an attempt to convince anyone of whether or not it works. *Feng shui* is a mixture of things: common sense, geographic and soil science, esoteric practices and perhaps superstition. Readers can decide for themselves what they wish to accept and what they wish to reject.

Chapters Two to Five specifically deal with aspects of *feng shui* as it is practised in Singapore.

In Chapter Six I discuss *feng shui* and attitudes to the environment which I consider to be of particular importance now, as we find ourselves faced with more and more serious environmental crises.

The academic conclusions of the study are set out in **Appendix One**. In adapting the thesis, some information has been omitted. This mainly consisted of the very specific discussion of research methods and statistical evaluations of information. The original thesis is entitled "The Professional Practice of Geomancy in Contemporary Singapore" and copies are held in the libraries of the University of Auckland, New Zealand and the National University of Singapore.

A bibliography of important sources is included at the end of the book. Brief references to these sources have occasionally been made in the text to indicate to the reader where further detail on a subject may be found.

Western commentaries on *feng shui* have appeared for more than one hundred years and it can now be seen that variations in the theory and practice of *feng shui* can occur with temporal or geographic distance from its traditional source. In this study, variation between the *feng shui* of traditional China and contemporary Singapore, and even between individual geomancers' ideas, is acknowledged rather than averaged. I believe that this is true to the nature of geomancy in contemporary Singapore and in its wider geographical and historical contexts. Growth and change in ideas can be prompted by varying circumstances, and the ability of *feng shui* to adapt to new conditions is part of its resilience. Singaporean *feng shui* is probably in transition at this time.

It is possible that by trying to do two things at once in this book (to produce both material of popular interest and information of use to academics) I have done neither terribly well. As with so much research, my initial questions have not led to answers, but to further questions. I cannot claim that this research is anything other than preliminary, but because there is so little information available about the actual practice of *feng shui* in Singapore I think it will be of interest to the increasing number of Chinese Singaporeans who are returning to many aspects of their culture and identity which have been submerged in Singapore's recent rush for economic development. I also hope it will at least indicate to academics the approximate nature of the discipline as it exists in contemporary Singapore. Perhaps it will prompt or even assist future research. Considerable further study is required before anything like a full understanding of *feng shui* in Singapore can be achieved.

Throughout the period of research for this study, in countless conversations with Singaporeans, the most common questions I faced were, "Do you believe in *feng shui*?" "Do you think it works?" In writing my thesis and this book I carefully avoided these questions on the basis that my role was to record rather than to judge. I do feel however that I should address this issue openly and state my prejudices while offering just a token of advice to the thoroughly confused once or future *feng shui* follower.

Firstly, I think it is obvious that much of *feng shui* is founded on common sense. Beyond that, some of the more abstruse aspects of *feng shui* practice can seem strange from a practical, rationalist point of view and I suspect that some elements of its current practice have been degraded through popular use. It is important to remember, though, that even modern physics cannot contain itself within purely rationalist boundaries and its leading edge sounds more and more like ancient Oriental wisdom as research progresses. I believe that *feng shui* is profoundly wise and should be treated with at least an open mind.

To those who intend to use it I say: educate yourselves a little. Read what you can about *feng shui* and decide what to accept and what to discard. If you do this and then choose a geomancer to advise you, after you have discussed his or her approaches, you should be confident in the advice and your subsequent actions.

There are many sad cases of geomantic hypochondria where people go from geomancer to geomancer constantly seeking new opinions, having no confidence in the advice obtained and living in fear of *feng shui* induced calamity. This is sad and very expensive! In fact these people lack confidence in themselves and allow *feng shui* to rule their lives in negative ways. If you are going to adopt *feng shui*, make it empower you and don't let it control you. *Feng shui* can enhance your life or confound it; it can be friend or foe.

The people I interviewed who seemed to have the greatest successes with *feng shui* were the ones who already had quite a clear idea of what they wanted in their lives. If a couple on the verge of divorce decide to give it one last try and consult a geomancer to good result, who can say whether it is the decision to make the marriage work and to let go of blame, or the reorientation of the front door and household furniture which has "worked"?

I have no doubt that both the environment and the person determine an individual's fate. To know yourself and to live in harmony with, indeed to identify with, the environment in all its forms is the surest road to success, fulfillment and happiness I can envisage. I believe it is also the surest way we have to save our planet, and ourselves along with it, from possible ecological collapse. In the depths of *feng shui* we can find guidance towards that kind of identification with nature and the environment, and through that we can discover our true selves.

* * *

My sincerest thanks go to:

- Dr Hong-key Yoon and Associate Professor Warwick Neville, both of the University of Auckland, for their help and encouragement.
- Professor George Parkyn, David Kirkpatrick, Birgitta Noble and Sarah Paterson for their advice and support.
- Mr Koh Kok Wah, for artistic help and general inspiration.
- David Ho Wing Leong and Debbie Chew for their assistance.

I am also particularly grateful to Master Danny Cheong, whose enthusiasm for this study and sincerity and dedication have been invaluable in helping to convince me that *feng shui* is a living philosophy in Singapore.

1
WHAT IS *FENG SHUI*?

When exploring Singapore, many people will puzzle over ornate figures of dragons, tigers and birds resting on the roof lines of buildings (**Photo 1**). They might see a small mirror or brush painting hanging over a doorway and a statue of a lion-like animal standing at either side (**Photo 2**). Those with an especially keen eye may notice that the entrances to some buildings are set at odd angles to the road. In the dealing room of a major bank, urns overflow with a mixture of salt and ink and desks stand at an odd angle to the walls. Features such as these are found scattered throughout Singapore. They may appear to be the random trappings of an ancient and rich culture, but they are more than that and far from random. The art that unifies all these details and gives them meaning is *feng shui*.

In its earliest beginnings in China, *feng shui*, or Chinese geomancy, was used to examine parts of the landscape to see if they might be appropriate places for occupation. If they were, then *feng shui* was also employed to determine the best position and arrangement of buildings. The ideas and practices of *feng shui* were based on early Chinese beliefs about cosmology or the structure of the universe and these ideas and beliefs have developed hand in hand for more than 3,000 years. *Feng shui* is a meeting place for mystic Chinese wisdom and everyday practicality.

While *feng shui* is still practised in Singapore today, it is more often used to adapt already specified sites to the needs of their existing occupiers than in the process of choosing a site in the first place. *Feng shui* is applied to help people make the best of what they have rather than to identify perfect locations. The practices employed in contemporary Singapore are, however, fundamentally the same as those used traditionally in China.

Feng shui remains popular in the countryside and in many cities in Asia, wherever Chinese influence is strong. It has travelled further abroad with Chinese migrations to the European-dominated world. Even some non-Chinese have adopted this ancient system of relating human existence to the environment as it has become established in the United States and fashionable in Paris.

The Meaning of *Feng Shui*

The English word "geomancy" literally means divination or fortune telling by examining the formations of the landscape. In this sense "geomancy" is quite a good, though limited, translation of *feng shui*. *Feng shui* encompasses more than just the reading of the earth's features. It is based on the belief that human fate and fortune is largely controlled or directed by cosmological forces. These are certainly considered to manifest themselves in the landscape but in *feng shui* both the landscape and the stars are directly consulted. According to these theories, careful analysis of a person's environment, both immediate and astrological, can reveal his or her fate.

The Chinese characters for *feng shui* 风水 can be translated directly as "wind and water". The practices of *feng shui* depend on careful examination of all the facets of the natural environment: wind and water represent a whole range of these. They are particularly important as representatives, however, because they suggest the dynamic condition of nature: the illusive, changeable but powerful character of the universe as perceived by the ancient Chinese. Together these two characters, *feng* (wind) and *shui* (water), symbolise the whole of Chinese cosmology and its philosophical and ethical foundations. Water in particular carries with it philosophical resonances. It is a symbol of hidden strength within apparent weakness. Lao Ze, an ancient philosopher (c. 600 BC) and the first master of Daoism (Taoism/*Dao Jia*), emphasised that although water dwells in lowly places and has no shape of its own it can overpower or undermine the strongest obstacles: buildings, cities or even mountains. A highly developed theory based on wind is also fundamental to Chinese medicine and anatomy. Excessive wind about various organs can be a danger to health and so must always be kept in balance with the other elements.

Like many disciplines of Chinese civilisation, which were never as exclusively defined as those of the Western tradition, *feng shui* rests on a broad interdisciplinary body of theory that developed over thousands of years. *Feng shui* incorporates ideas of geography, aesthetics, ecology, psychology, astrology and more. It has been applied through many generations to widely varying circumstances and has proved capable of considerable adaption under new conditions or in the hands of a new master. Though this variation has led to differing interpretations of *feng shui*, its central concepts survive.

Modern commentators also differ in their approaches to *feng shui*. Because the system is wide-ranging, people can easily see in it what they set out to see. Some definitions emphasise the aspirations of the *feng shui* consumer: the pursuit of happiness and prosperity and the belief that the achievement of these is dependant on environmental influences. Others focus on the way in which *feng shui* represents attitudes to the environment and how it has played a part in limiting human impact on nature in places such as China, Hong Kong and Korea. Although these approaches are correct, they result in only partial definitions. A complete understanding of *feng shui* cannot be distilled into a single paragraph.

In Singapore, the most widely-known aspect of *feng shui* is its use in establishing the most beneficial orientation of buildings and the arrangement of their furniture. This has been the main focus of Singaporean literature on *feng shui*, but again it is only part of the picture. In this book I hope to provide a fuller description of what *feng shui* is and does in contemporary Singapore.

Traditionally, *feng shui* was used to ensure that the construction of buildings and other changes to the natural environment would be carried out in the best places and most appropriate ways (according to its own standards). In contemporary Singapore, however, the emphasis has been reversed. Singaporean geomancers are most often employed to examine buildings that are already owned or occupied by their clients. The task of the geomancer under these circumstances is to adjust the way the building and its occupants interact with the environment, by careful arrangement of furniture and fittings, so that negative forces are deflected and positive forces enhanced. The difference seems subtle but is actually quite fundamental. This will be discussed more fully in later chapters. First, it is important to provide a more thorough explanation of the origins and principles of *feng shui*.

The Origins of *Feng Shui*

Feng shui as a system consists of several different theories and ideas. Because of this, its origin cannot be traced back to a single source in Chinese history. Some of the most important ideas of Chinese philosophy and natural law, such as the *yin-yang*, five elements and eight trigrams theories, are fundamental to *feng shui*. It also encompasses theories of the ideal landscape that are used to analyse landforms and watercourses. Each of these ideas is a substantial body of thought in itself, but all are closely interwoven in the practices of *feng shui*.

The theory of the ideal landscape has been discussed by a number of authors who do not always agree about its possible origin. In *feng shui*, the dwelling places of the living and the dead (houses and graves) should be located according to the principles of the ideal landscape. Some authors argue that the concepts of the ideal site would have been applied to graves first because of the strong emphasis on ancestor worship in traditional Chinese society. From there, they argue, the practices would have been extended to sites for the living.

Other scholars consider that *feng shui* for graves would have evolved out of that applied to sites for the living. A very convincing argument is put forward by Dr Hong-key Yoon, who states that it is instinctive for all species to seek out places to live that most suit their specific needs. It is likely that the methods of landscape analysis found in *feng shui* grew from this. Consequently, Dr Yoon argues that *feng shui* would have been applied to houses first and was subsequently extended to locating auspicious grave sites.

The origin of the principles of the ideal landscape is likely to have been among the ancient cave dwellers of the Loess Plateau of Central China[1]. This area is considered to be the cradle of Chinese civilisation. Cave dwelling is a widespread and very practical way of living which has been practised there for thousands of years and continues to this day. The landscape features recommended in the theory of the ideal landscape correspond exactly with those required for a comfortable and safe cave in that area. Furthermore, the word used in *feng shui* literature to denote the ideal site is "cave" (*xue*).

In general, the conditions of the ideal geomantic landscape are very logical requirements for a comfortable house in any of the cooler regions of the northern hemisphere (emphasising, among other things, a southerly aspect) and this must go some way to explaining why the system has taken hold throughout the Chinese world.

The origins of Chinese theories of cosmology are also obscure, being so

---

[1] Yoon, 1986.

ancient that accurate historical records are very scarce. Some of the earliest systematic accounts in Chinese literature of the structure of the universe are found in the first Daoist writings such as the *Dao De Jing* by Lao Ze, dating from about 600 BC. Lao Ze's description of the universe has been the basis of subsequent developments in Chinese cosmology and is fundamental to the theories of *feng shui*.

One of the most important concepts shared by Chinese cosmology and *feng shui* is the idea of dynamic balance in the universe. In its simplest form, Chinese cosmology is represented by the symbol of the Great Ultimate (*Taiji*), commonly known as the *yin-yang* symbol (**Fig. 1**). The symbol of the Great Ultimate is a visual representation of *Dao*. *Dao* is the undefinable unity behind all things and can be literally translated as "Road" or "Way". *Dao* is holistic; all parts of it are interrelated and interdependent. It is not an anthropomorphic god; instead, *dao* is the motive principle behind all existence.

Dao encompasses *yin* and *yang*: negative and positive forces represented by the black and white sections of the symbol respectively. These are value-free opposites, conveying senses of (among other things): yielding and strong, dark and light, cold and heat, female and male. However, each opposite in a pair is not considered to be entirely exclusive of the other. In fact, Lao Ze considered such distinctions to be illusory, merely

*Fig. 1. The symbol of **Taiji** – the Great Ultimate.*

fabrications of the human mind. Within both *yin* and *yang* are the seeds of their opposites. At its extreme, *yang* becomes *yin* and *yin* becomes *yang* and thus the universe is in a constant state of movement and transmutation. Through the mixing of *yin* and *yang* within *dao* the "10,000 things" (*wan wu* – that is, "all things") are created. Humanity is but one of the 10,000 things.

Other powerful forces within *dao* are seen to guide the flux of the universe. However, in contrast with Western cosmology, these forces which form basic natural laws to the Chinese are more akin to philosophical principles than to descriptions of the material building blocks of the world. To ancient Chinese theorists, the laws of nature were processes and cycles rather than categories of physical substance.

The concepts of *li* and *qi* also became very important in the Chinese understanding of the universe. *Li* is the principle behind, or the blueprint of, all the facets of the universe. *Qi* is the energy that invests principle or form with life. To explain *qi*, a Singaporean geomancer uses the analogy of an electric source powering a computer. Without electricity a computer is a useless mass of wires and plastic; without life force a bird is mere tissue and the universe is nothing.

Qi is often translated into English as 'vital energy'. The accumulation of beneficial *qi* in a site is the primary aim of all geomantic practice. Beneficial *qi* is called *sheng qi*, while destructive *qi* is called *sha qi*.

The eight trigrams (*ba gua*) and the five elements (*wu xing*) theories are also essential elements of Chinese cosmology and *feng shui* practice. The five elements (wind, water, fire, earth and metal) appear to be a basic list of types of physical substance, but this is due to general acceptance of an inadequate translation. *Wu* is indeed the number five, but *xing* is literally "movement", so a more accurate translation might be "five forces". I will continue to use "five elements" in this text, however, as it is now the standard translation.

The five elements are usually presented in two different arrangements, as either the cycle of mutual creation or the cycle of mutual destruction (**Fig. 2**). These two cycles are not merely the reverse of each other, but are entirely different sequences. They are organised so that any possible pair of elements corresponds with one and only one of the cycles. For example, fire and metal together are part of the cycle of destruction as

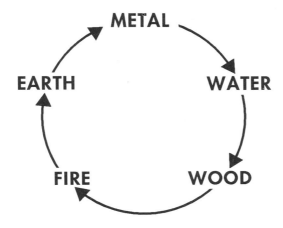

CYCLE OF ELEMENTS PRODUCING EACH OTHER

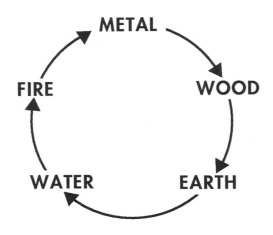

CYCLE OF ELEMENTS DESTROYING EACH OTHER

Fig. 2. The two cycles of the five elements.

according to five elements theory fire destroys metal, while fire and earth are part of the cycle of creation as fire creates earth. Because every person, landform or other thing is associated with one of the elements, the relationship between any two things will be dominated by either the creative or destructive cycle. Consequently, analysis of a person's surroundings according to the compatibility of the elements of individual features is a central part of *feng shui* practice.

The eight trigrams, which were already well established for use in divination by Lao Ze's time, are associated with the theory of changes as described in the *I Jing* or *Book of Changes*. Numerology, astrology and divination based on the eight trigrams were three of the so-called Six Occult Arts. These occult arts are largely associated with fortune telling and are still fairly commonly practised today. The three mentioned are very important in *feng shui* as it is practised in Singapore. Many modern geomancers will provide services such as recommending auspicious names for newborn babies and dates for undertaking important events as well as giving geomantic advice. In fact, this is so common that most Singaporeans do not distinguish between geomancy, astrology and numerology and will refer to them together as *feng shui*.

The eight trigrams probably developed out of a form of divination which dates from the Shang dynasty (otherwise known as the Yin dynasty, c.1766 – c.1123 BC). A fortune teller would leave the shoulder blade of an ox or a tortoise shell in the sun until it became dry and cracked. Then, interpreting the arrangement of broken and unbroken lines, the fate of the person or endeavour would be predicted. It seems likely that this practice developed into the method of divination described in the *I Jing* which is based essentially on the eight trigrams.

Each trigram is made up of three lines that are either broken or unbroken. Unbroken lines are *yang* (strong) and broken ones *yin* (yielding). Using the two types of line in the three different positions, eight possible trigrams can be made. Each trigram is named after and represents a force or process in the universe. *Chien*, made up of three *yang* lines, is "the Creative" while *Kun*, consisting of three *yin* lines, is "the Receptive". The intermediate trigrams that contain a mixture of *yin* and *yang* lines are considered to be relatively *yin* or *yang* depending on their structure.

Like the five elements, the eight trigrams are presented in two different ways, the Earlier or Former Heaven Arrangement and the Later Heaven Arrangement (**Fig. 3**), but these are not cycles. The Former Heaven Arrangement is considered to show the trigrams in their ideal or heavenly configuration and this is usually the arrangement found on the talismanic mirrors used in *feng shui* to deflect *sha qi*. The Later Heaven Arrangement represents the trigrams as they are seen to operate on earth. In both cases, each trigram is associated with one of the eight main points of the compass (north, north-east, east, south-east etc.) and the two arrangements are fundamental and essential divisions appearing on the *feng shui* compass or *luo pan*.

The orientation of buildings and their furnishings is one of the most important functional aspects of *feng shui*. A fundamental way in which the Chinese conceptualise physical space is in terms of five directions: north, south, east, west and centre. Each of these is associated with one of the elements and a colour (**Fig. 4**). Sometimes the reason behind an association seems intuitively obvious. For instance, south is associated with the element "fire" and the colour "red". This probably relates to the south being the direction (from China) to the equator, warmth and the sun in winter. The centre is associated with "earth" and "yellow"; while this symbolism is found throughout Chinese culture its basis is more obscure. It quite probably originated in the Loess Plateau which is considered to be the cradle of Chinese civilisation and where the yellow loess soil dominates the landscape and the lives of the agrarian population.

The association of the five elements and the eight trigrams with the cardinal directions is only the beginning. As well as these, the hours, days, months and years (and therefore people's dates of birth), shapes of hills and mountains, plants, animals and various mental and physical states are all associated with the directions, hexagrams and elements. This complex web of interrelationships is the basis of the analysis of harmony and conflict between humans and the natural environment.

Further associations with the directions that are found on the *luo pan* and constitute a detailed description of the Chinese cosmological order are carefully explained by Stephen Skinner[2]. These include the Ten Heavenly Stems, the 12 Earthly Branches, the Sexagenary Characters and the 120 *Fen Chin*, each of which relates to astrological points and

---

[2] Skinner, 1983.

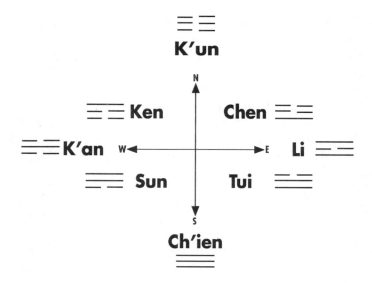

EARLIER OR FORMER HEAVEN ARRANGEMENT

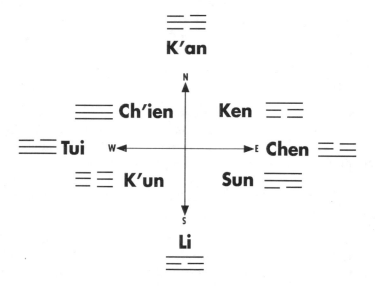

LATER HEAVEN ARRANGEMENT

Fig. 3. The two arrangements of the eight trigrams.

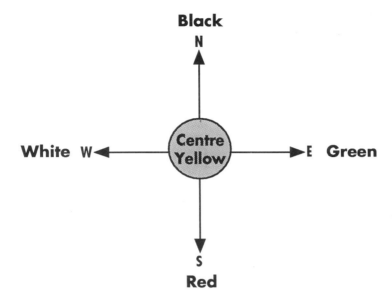

Fig. 4. The colour associations of the five directions.

positions, flow of *qi* and of course both time and place. The 12 Earthly branches are also associated with the animals of the Chinese zodiac.

The elements and hexagrams associated with the date and time of birth of a person are the key to his or her relationship with the surrounding environment. Through analysis of the directions, elements and other cosmological categories, the relationship of just about any two objects in the environment, or any object and a person, can be seen to be creative or destructive, harmonious or conflicting.

With the *luo pan*, the geomancer can carefully determine how the various features of the environment interact in terms of the elements and hexagrams and whether or not they will be beneficial or destructive for the occupant. The geomancer also employs a geomantic ruler to help determine the auspiciousness of the dimensions of rooms, furniture, doors and the like.

According to this analysis of the universe, the relationship in space and time of all things to each other and to every person is determined by natural law. All human structures are part of nature and the fate of people and their activities are, as a matter of course, profoundly affected by the environment in which they exist. Humanity is merely a part of a vast network of objects and forces. Individually and collectively, human lives and conditions are determined by these environmental influences and also act as environmental influences. Consequently, the careful arrangement of structures within the environment becomes a powerful tool enabling people to exert some control over their lives. This is the primary aim of *feng shui*.

The Two Schools of *Feng Shui*

The role of the geomancer is to analyse the influences the environment has on the client and adjust them so that beneficial forces prevail and the site receives abundant *sheng qi*. Two different approaches can be employed to do this and these are related to the two schools of *feng shui*, the Form School and the Compass School.

In fact, the methods of these two schools are usually applied in combination by most geomancers and are quite closely related. The Form School focuses on the physical arrangement of the landscape, hills, flatlands and rivers to find inherently auspicious sites. The Compass School uses the detailed analysis of the directions, elements, hexagrams etc. to determine the influences on the site.

The Compass School

The elements and trigrams associated with the person's time and date of birth must harmonise with the physical environment and the most important medium which guides this is orientation. The orientation of any feature of a building determines what universal forces it is subject to. For example, the main door to a building is described as the *qi kou*, literally "energy mouth", by Singaporean geomancer George Koh. *Qi*, the animating energy of the universe, is said to enter a building through the main door; it can be likened to a person's nose, which is the entrance for life giving air to the human body. Because of this, the direction of the main door, which determines the quality of the *qi* admitted by it, will have a profound effect on the fate of the occupants. Likewise, a person's bed should be positioned so that it is subject to rejuvenating *qi* and not conflicting forces.

The orientation of these and other key features of the building such as, for a home, the cooker, ancestral altar, sink and toilet, and for an office, the reception area and desks, all affect the kind of influences that will prevail over the people who use the premises. Outside the building, the directions to main roads and intersections, large buildings and other dominant landscape features also determine whether the building is subject to *sheng qi* or *sha qi*.

If positive influences are harnessed and negative influences are deflected then the situation is considered to be harmonious. The cycle of production will dominate the place and result in health and wealth, happiness and success for the family or business. If negative influences or conflict between elements dominate then evil fortune, ill health or confusion will descend on the occupants. These consequences are considered to be inevitable as they are the direct results of the laws of nature.

In contemporary Singapore these methods, which are associated with the Compass School, are the main components of *feng shui* practice. Most geomancers consider that through the careful use of the compass methods and manipulation of the features of the site, almost any building can be organised so that the environmental influences will be beneficial or, at the very least, not detrimental. Furniture is placed in areas where rich sources of *sheng qi* flow. Talismans and remedies are used where *sha qi* is found.

The most common remedies involve the strategic placement of objects that are considered to have some geomantic power. Often these will be nature paintings, statues, figurines, written talismans or mirrors that are surrounded by the eight trigrams. These are placed over doors and in other places where *sha qi* is considered to be influential. These symbols, often powerful images from nature, are believed to affect the place by either producing *sheng qi* or deflecting *sha qi*. A sculpture of a lion or a painting of a tiger somehow embodies the power or essence of the living creature; the ideal Former Heaven arrangement of the eight trigrams contains those ideal forces to some extent and each can convey these influences to the environment.

A geomancer related the story of one of his clients, a successful businessperson whose company had suddenly begun to decline. On examining the premises, the geomancer discovered that his client had hung a painting of a ferocious tiger in his office opposite the door. The geomancer considered that every day, on entering his office, the client was being "bitten and overpowered by the tiger". Once the painting was removed, the company recovered.

In Western terms, this area of *feng shui* delves into the world of magic and even among geomancers there is some debate about the efficacy of these practices. Some will argue that these symbols are mysteriously and powerfully linked to the forces of nature while others consider their influences to be based in psychology and environmental aesthetics. Regardless, the use of talismans is an important tool associated with the compass methods of *feng shui*.

The Form School

The Form School, which is complementary to the Compass School, focuses on the physical shapes and configurations of the landscape to find sites that are most likely to bring good fortune for the occupants. In its simplest form, the ideal landscape consists of a range of hills or mountains making a curve in the shape of a "u" or horseshoe. In early Chinese depictions of the ideal landscape, south was at the top of the page and north at the bottom, the reverse of the Western convention. The horseshoe-shaped mountain range would be open at the top where there would be flat lands and beyond them a meandering stream. The perfect site in this ideal landscape would be found somewhere in the middle of the curve of hills, where the slope was not too steep. This basic pattern is sometimes called "*zuo shan xiang hai*" or "sitting on a mountain facing the sea" and is the foundation for all of the more complex descriptions of ideal landscapes.

The eastern side of the horseshoe is referred to as the "azure dragon" and the western side is the "white tiger"; where the two meet is sometimes called the "black tortoise" or simply the "main mountain". The azure dragon is considered to embody mainly *yang* force while the white tiger is *yin*. At the point where they meet, at the cave or *xue*, a perfect blend of *yin* and *yang* is supposed to exist and so the most beneficial kind of *sheng qi* is abundant. In classical Chinese texts the analogy of sexual intercourse was sometimes used to describe this landscape configuration and the forces of *yang* and *yin* were associated with the male and female respectively.

The landscape has to meet a further set of specific criteria to be considered ideal (**Fig. 5**). The horseshoe-shaped range should be unbroken as its main function is to protect the ideal site from cold winds from the east, west

Fig. 5. The Ideal Landscape.

and particularly the north. A smaller mountain called the "red bird" may be found to the south for further protection, but this should not be too close to the ideal site or joined to the enclosing mountain range as it might obstruct access or sunlight. These features of the landscape are considered most important as they protect the cave from wind (*feng*) and provide it with water (*shui*). They also provide an easily defended territory. On this level the ideal geomantic landscape seems firmly grounded in common sense.

Mountains and mountain ranges in general are called "*long*" which is commonly translated as "dragon", though this mythical animal is more like a cross between a dragon and a snake. The most auspicious ranges of hills or mountains should undulate gently and evenly like the back of such an animal. In its most strict requirements, the azure dragon should be slightly larger than the white tiger as, in ideal proportions, *yang* should slightly outweigh *yin*[3]. The whole system is often depicted as a dragon and a tiger, or two dragons, holding a pearl between them or playing with a ball. The pearl or ball, of course, corresponds with the ideal site.

Soil quality and vegetation are also considered to be very important. The ideal soil type is described as fine in texture, firm in structure and yellow in colour and can be likened to soybean flour. This soil was considered to be resistant to white ants, which could otherwise infest a grave and destroy the bones of a buried ancestor, thus depriving the descendants of any of the benefits that the use of a geomantically perfect site should bring them. These characteristics are also thought to originate from the Loess Plateau[4].

Consistent with its holistic and universal nature, *sheng qi* is beneficial to all forms of life in *feng shui*. Lush vegetation indicates a place that is rich in vital energy, where people will prosper and buried ancestors will rest comfortably (death being just another stage of life) and direct good fortune

---

[3] The idea that there should be slightly more *yang* than *yin* for proportions to be perfect is probably a later addition to *feng shui* theory. Lao Ze considered perfect balance between *yin* and *yang* to be most important and certainly did not indicate that either should dominate. In later Daoist writings, the tendency to favour *yang* developed and I believe that this reflects the prejudice towards the masculine of later philosophers. Lao Ze himself considered the female principle to be the perfect balance to the male principle and sometimes argued that it be favoured e.g. "Know the *yang* but keep to the *yin*."

[4] Yoon, 1986.

to their descendants. A Singaporean geomancer also considered the requirement of lush vegetation at an ideal site to be founded on logic as a forested hill would provide fuel for fires and animals to catch:

> "... in China the north wind is very cold, the mountain blocks the wind and you don't get sick at winter time. You want to be close to the mountain because you need to chop wood to burn, there are animals you can trap. You need to be near to water to wash your rice and vegetables and clothes. Being near the mountain, the fertile earth washes down for you to grow crops. Isn't that good living when you are talking about one to two hundred years ago in the village?"

One essential factor lies at the heart of all the various requirements of the ideal landscape and that is the accumulation of *sheng qi*. *Qi* in the form of vital energy was traditionally thought to flow only underground. Wind could disperse *sheng qi* into the air and once out of the ground it would transform into wind, cloud or rain. So, to retain its beneficial qualities, the ground that *qi* flowed through had to be protected from wind and this is one of the ideas underlying the requirement of sheltering mountains. Because *qi* flows through the ground the terrain itself was considered to be indicative of the quality of *qi* flowing through it.

As with many early civilisations, the ancient Chinese considered their empire to be at the physical centre of the universe. Hence in its own language, China was and still is Zhongguo ("middle kingdom"). The Kun Lun mountains of China, which lead up to the Tibetan Plateau, were considered to be the backbone of the universe from which all mountain ranges radiated. They were also thought to be the source of all *qi*. *Qi* flows from the Kun Lun mountains out and down through other mountain ranges like blood running through the veins of dragons or sap through the branches of trees. The image of fruit in the branches of a tree or berries on a vine was sometimes used as an analogy for the location of auspicious places, which accumulate *sheng qi*, among the mountain ranges.

The ideas behind using ideal geomantic sites for burial are also based on the intention to accumulate *qi*. From the earliest times, the Chinese have embraced the doctrines of ancestor worship and filial piety. Because life and death are not so rigidly separated in the Chinese tradition as in the West, the dead are considered to be able to directly affect the lives of the living. Whether for the benefit of their ancestors or themselves, people believed the comfort of the dead to be extremely important.

One explanation of the relationship between the living and the dead is based on the transmission of *qi*. *Qi* flowing through the ground and into the bones of a buried ancestor was thought to be transmitted directly to the living descendants and so the abundance of *sheng qi* available to a grave could have a profound effect on the fortunes of living descendants. A Singaporean geomancer explained that ancestors and descendants are linked in an energy field through which the buried ancestor transmits energy to the living descendant. If the ancestor is buried in a place rich in *sheng qi*, the flesh of the corpse will decay rapidly but the bones will be well preserved and health, prosperity and luck will flow to the descendants.

As the animating force of the universe, all objects in nature depend on the availability of *sheng qi* and in a sense all things are considered to be alive. This idea corresponds with recent radical extensions of Western theories of ecology (and developments in other sciences such as quantum physics), going further than even the Gaia philosophy in which the earth and its atmosphere are seen to be a living, self-regulating whole.

In *feng shui*, landscapes are also interpreted as integrated living systems. For a landscape to be alive, it would require all the features required in life. Well-known examples include that of a village in the form of a sleeping ox where a particular outcrop of rocks constituted the ox's food.

Changes to the natural order of the environment could only be made with great caution, as disturbance of a feature of the living landscape could bring calamity to a community. If the rocks forming food for the ox were taken away, the ox would die. If wells were haphazardly dug in a village having the image of a sailing boat, the village would sink[5]. Traditionally, this facet of *feng shui* could regulate the behaviour of people in their environments quite strictly and in this way *feng shui* could be considered a tool for environmental protection[6]. There are many similar examples to be found in the research conducted in China, Hong Kong and Korea, and such living landscapes are also a part of the geomantic folklore of Singapore.

---

[5] Yoon, 1976.
[6] Yoon, 1976.

2
THE GEOMANCERS AND THEIR BUSINESSES

There is no doubt that *feng shui* is influential to some degree in Singapore. It seems that most Singaporeans know of *feng shui* and a growing number have an interest in its principles, although those who actively seek to use *feng shui* may still be a relatively small minority. Certainly there are amateur and lay geomancers, but it is in the professional practice that geomancy attains its highest profile and purest form in Singapore.

The geomancer-client relationship is central to this type of geomantic practice. Many geomancers and clients liken the relationship of practitioner and client to that of a doctor and patient. This in itself illustrates the particular character of geomancy in Singapore: it tends to be used to fix problems rather than to prevent them. Regardless of this, professional geomancers are the focus of, and in many ways the driving force behind, *feng shui* practice in Singapore.

Ten professional geomancers were interviewed in detail for this book (see **Appendix Two**). These included three out of four of the most prominent professional geomancers in practice at the time.

Geomancers' Backgrounds

The great majority of the geomancers interviewed had become interested in *feng shui* in their adult lives. Most had held other jobs before deciding to practice geomancy, but all remembered hearing about *feng shui* during their childhood years. Only three had taken much notice at that stage.

One was strongly influenced by his father who was a geomancer. During his childhood he spent time watching and learning from his father who practised part-time in Singapore. The geomancer's father was also friendly with the late geomancer-monk Reverend Hong Chun. Reverend Hong Chun apparently passed some written material on to the father and later introduced some clients to the son. This indicates a very special relationship between the Reverend and this pair, as other geomancers believe that Reverend Hong Chun chose not to train any apprentices because he felt that most people practised geomancy purely out of self-interest. The son in this case has been practising as a geomancer now for over ten years.

Another geomancer hadn't thought much about *feng shui* until he was a teenager, when he had a dream about meeting an old man who would change his life. Soon afterwards, he ran into this man on the street and they felt strongly as if they knew each other. The old man was a lay geomancer and taught the young man his skills. The younger geomancer has been practising in his own business now for about three years.

The third was brought up in the Fu Jian province of China and had become interested in *feng shui* because he had seen it in use in his village. He became an apprentice to two *feng shui* masters in Fu Jian and studied under them for three years. Later, he moved to Singapore and has been practising as a geomancer for 15 years.

These three stories illustrate how the discipline of *feng shui* has traditionally been handed from master to apprentice down through generations (though not necessarily through families). In Singapore, however, this situation is less common. All the other geomancers learnt their skills through studying books, attending classes and seminars and visiting masters outside Singapore for comparatively short periods of time. Some also adopted other traditional Chinese practices such as meditation and *qi gong*.

Interestingly, all the geomancers interviewed were very firm that *feng shui* is not a religious practice or particularly associated with a religion. Among the geomancers there were Buddhists, Daoists, followers of the Goddess of Mercy (who appears in both Buddhism and Daoism) and Christians.

Studies in other countries have shown a close relationship between Buddhism and *feng shui*. For example, Yoon's work establishes the common phenomenon of the monk-geomancer in Korea. In Singapore, the boundary between Buddhism and Daoism can be somewhat vague and many Singaporeans say that they practise "Chinese Religion" which comprises parts of each along with other esoteric Chinese beliefs. Many of the surviving early Chinese temples are located in very auspicious places and some even display original plaques which attribute the choice of site to geomantic principles[1].

---

[1] Lip, 1979.

Feng shui has perhaps adopted some religious principles. Many geomancers believe that the character of a person, particularly that person's virtuousness, can affect how well *feng shui* will work. A bad person may not get any benefit from *feng shui*, or it might work for a while and then stop. Nevertheless this is very different from saying that *feng shui* is part of Chinese religion, as has been claimed by some previous Western interpreters. *Feng shui* is based on a cosmology that has developed hand in hand with the Chinese religions but in itself is not really a religion any more than Hawking's Quantum Theory of Gravity is. In modern day Singapore it is more accurate to say that *feng shui* is part of the Chinese world view. Certainly this world view is partly a product of Chinese religion but the practice of *feng shui* is not dependant on belief in a Chinese, or any other, religion. In more traditional environments there would usually be an accepted hierarchy of geomancers where a few are considered to be the most senior or scholarly – the true masters. Below this, there would be younger (though still quite accomplished) geomancers through to the apprentices and assistants. In Yoon's study of geomancy in Korea, he found that all the most respected geomancers were over the age of 50.

There is quite a lack of these senior geomancers in Singapore. Reverend Hong Chun was the only person who really fulfilled this role, yet he did not formally take apprentices. By the time of his death, in his 80s or possibly 90s, the Reverend had achieved almost legendary status. This study was carried out very shortly before he died and unfortunately he declined to be interviewed. Many Singaporean geomancers considered him to be the pre-eminent practitioner of *feng shui* in Singapore, Malaysia and Indonesia. He was rumoured to be a personal adviser to the then Prime Minister, Lee Kuan Yew, and there are stories that he determined the layout for the MRT (Mass Rapid Transit underground rail network) and prescribed the construction of the Merlion statue at the entrance to the Singapore River, both on geomantic grounds. Of course, there is no evidence that any of this is true but it does illustrate the degree of prominence and authority attributed to him.

Another difficulty with this whole subject is that it is often considered improper to ask a geomancer his or her age. Consequently such questions had to be asked very carefully and usually the answers were somewhat vague. "In my 30s" was the most common answer to my cautious question.

Only one of the geomancers interviewed was over 50 and, though highly respected, cannot really be considered a grand master in traditional terms because of a relative lack of experience.

The four most prominent full-time geomancers in Singapore are all in their late 30s and 40s. These four advertise regularly in the newspapers and are often referred to in television programmes and other media. All of this is quite unconventional in traditional terms: some geomancers feel that self advertisement is against the spirit of *feng shui* – if you are good, work should just come to you.

The youngest of these four is extremely business-oriented and is very active in promoting his practice through lectures, exhibitions and advertisements. His approach is very untraditional, both in its business drive and in some of his theories. Though his background is quite traditional, he is very much a self-styled modern geomancer who has even adopted some relatively high-technology approaches into his practice. He has acted as consultant to a number of large commercial organisations and has given advice to several businesses moving into the geomantically controversial Gateway development.

All the remaining geomancers were also under 50; the youngest was 26 at the time of the interview. Clearly the hierarchy of geomancers in Singapore is very bottom heavy. This is one of many pieces of evidence which lead me to believe that there has been a relatively recent upsurge of interest in *feng shui* in Singapore. It appears to have started between one and two decades ago and has really gained in popularity in the last five years.

Nine of the ten geomancers interviewed are full ethnic Chinese while one is part Chinese and part Malay. The almost total lack of assimilation of non-Chinese into the discipline is noteworthy but unsurprising. Most of the geomancers had family origins in the coastal area of China, from Fu Jian province and further south, which is where most Singaporean Chinese come from. This area is also particularly associated with the Compass School of *feng shui* that definitely dominates its practice in Singapore.

Interviews with the Geomancers

The next few pages consist of some small excerpts from interviews with geomancers who participated in the study. I have selected the quotes in the hope that something of the personalities of the geomancers will come through, so that readers can gain some insight into their beliefs, hopes and problems. Some of their ideas conflict, but many are shared.

The interviews were all conducted in person and taped so, of course, the language used is not as formal or contrived as written English. I have transcribed them here with as little editing as possible so that the geomancers' own words and meanings are not subjected to my interpretation. Also native speakers of British or American English should bear in mind that Singaporean English can be quite different to theirs and will seem unusual to them. This is a chance to hear the geomancers speaking for themselves.

> "When I was about 13, I dreamed about an old man. I dreamed I would find him and that he would teach me everything and that I was born to learn these things. Soon after, I saw him and I felt I knew him well. He was just walking down the street and we felt we had to talk to each other. My master worked as a hawker at a food centre and only practised *feng shui* part time. Now he is more than 70 years old. He only does it for some people. Not for money. He is Teochew, came from China to Singapore when he was 34 . . .
>
> "Since I was 14 or 15 I would go to houses and cemeteries with him. He taught me from books and from experience. I went with him until I went to technical college to study engineering. But after that I decided to practise *feng shui* full time. My master taught me for the first three years I should not charge. Now, for two years I have been running my *feng shui* business."

> "There is a saying: First is birth, second is luck, third is geomancy, fourth is kindness, fifth is studies. Studies are least important of the five. If you are born rich there is no need to study. If your luck is right that is very good, but a geomancer can make it better; if it's no good to start, geomancy can make it better. It can tilt our lives. Kindness works on your life slowly, you don't get immediate returns. Study can improve your life through a good job. One of the things that can change your life is geomancy. You see there is no religion in this saying. Even so, Chinese are keen on religion whether they

are official followers or practise half past six religion. This saying kindled my interest in *feng shui* . . .

"Also when I was young, I heard stories. There were two families living in Coleman St opposite each other. One got in a geomancer and in the end it caused tragedy. The geomancer said that the family's luck was blocked by the house opposite. Perhaps this was true but what remedy is there? They put up a *ba gua* to reflect the building off. The people on the other side put up something bigger to shine it back. In the end one family brought in a black magician and then there was war between two black magicians. We knew someone who lived next door who was worried that flying black magic might hit his house so he sold out. Both of the families suffered ill fate. One family had many daughters and only one son. Some of the daughters went mad, some blind. Again I thought – is geomancy so powerful? But I did not want to get involved.

"Later I was working as a social worker but I didn't feel I could really make a difference to people's lives, to really solve their problems. Also I am a Buddhist, am studying to be an official Buddhist. I follow the Mahayana school because I believe in helping people. So then I thought I could help people more by practising geomancy. If you practise geomancy carefully and in good heart you won't do such evil things. I went to Hong Kong to study and now I have been practising for two years . . .

"What kind of people come to see me? I think there are three types. Firstly, people who are already in trouble. *Feng shui* can make problems if it is not alright. Some people might go to a monk. Maybe they have psychological trouble or business problems so they try a geomancer. Another kind is people who don't have troubles. Things are good but they want to be better and pass it on to the next generation. Third are people who don't want trouble to come . . .

"Mostly people have family problems, they quarrel with their loved ones or there is trouble with the children. There is a whole range of degrees. There may be problems with the job, for instance, not getting a rise . . .

"I had a client who moved house. The owner who sold it to him was a friend. There were problems with the house and they became enemies. The new owner's wife and children had all fallen sick but not the owner. He thought there could be a curse from the previous owner or perhaps the *feng shui* was not okay. The first stage is feeling miserable, like things are not on your wavelength. The second stage is an illness you have never had before. The last stage is serious illness, paralysis or even death . . .

"Whether premises suit you or not is very important. For instance Lucky Plaza, it is one of the most expensive buildings along with Parkway, Wisma[2] etc. The dragon is there but some people don't make money. Why? The elements of the person don't suit the elements of the unit. This is very, very important. Even if you are in Parkway Parade or you have a sea view, if your business drops it's likely the new place doesn't suit your elements which go with your birth year. When selecting a unit, the first person to look at it should be the geomancer. If it suits you then he will work out where to sit etc. then you bring in the contractors . . .

"Geomancy is coming up fast in Singapore but still people prefer to get the house first then see a geomancer. Strength of belief in *feng shui* is the key, like belief in religion. If you are looking for a new job you may go to church or the temple to pray for the right job. If you believed in *feng shui* you would go to the geomancer first and ask him to check out your home, or even ask him to help find your premises. In some places the geomancer is like a broker. Most Singaporeans are not at this stage . . .

"I try to make geomancy and beauty work together. Sometimes it is not possible, the table must be put in a position which is odd. If you are really serious about *feng shui* you must be prepared for this. Maybe I will have to recommend that you paint your front door black. Those who do not follow a geomancer's advice – ten percent of them are playing with their own lives . . .

"*Qi* is a force like air or whatever. Most people can't see it but a good geomancer can see it, or more it is to feel it, from high places at dawn where there are no structures. You can tell just like with polluted air. You can tell where the good and the bad air are. Geomancers, and maybe other people too, can sense where are the

---

[2] Parkway Parade near East Coast Parkway and Wisma Atria on Orchard Road.

good places and where are the bad. You can sense the *sha qi*. Early in the morning is important, this is when it is clearest. You can feel the *qi* because you feel better in it. But again it also depends on the elements: the east coast may suit you better than the west coast because of the elements . . .

"In order for *feng shui* to work fully, three parts must be fulfilled. First is the ancestral tombstones, second is home and third is work. If the ancestors are buried correctly there will be very, very bright descendants, the old *feng shui* practices were meant for that. If your home is good it will help you know what is good and bad, if your work place is bad the *feng shui* is stuck so for it to work perfectly work must also be good . . .

"Now that most people are cremated it is the ancestral tombstones that are important. The very first Cheongs, the very first Tans, if their tombstones are in good places, all the Cheongs and Tans will benefit. Nowadays home is the true base so the house is very important, then work. But if you want your children and grandchildren to be good you can find a good piece of land to bury yourself. *Feng shui* works in a way you can't see but you can feel it. I tell my clients: when your business or house is done even your regular clients may not give you business. The reason is that *feng shui* will help you throw away lousy clients. These will be the bad payers, the fussy ones, the ones who want money under the table. It will help you bring in new clients. . .

"*Feng shui* is also to do with your conscience, if you use it to bad ends it can't last. The approach has to be to help people around you. Otherwise the next generation will suffer, that is why some people are born with afflictions such as blindness. If this life is bad for you, get the geomancer in to balance it back. With good geomancy and good heart it will work faster, longer, better. If you are bad, it will not last."

"*Feng shui* has become much more popular in the last ten years or so and it is getting more and more popular, but people here are still not crazy about it the way Hong Kong people are. It is still developing and people are still learning about it. Unlike Hong Kong people or even Jakarta people who never argue with you about the price because they believe, here in Singapore they will try to bargain you down, they are conservative and calculative. It is like the doctor. You don't go to the doctor and bargain over price. Only when they have great trouble will they come and ask what can you offer me. They don't plan in advance. Whereas the Hong Kong people, when they move office, right at the beginning they get you in to make sure from the start. They feel they have to get the *feng shui* done. That is why I don't concentrate on the local market. Often it takes really big trouble, maybe the bank wants to repossess the business or the marriage is on the rocks, then they come, like going to the doctor, and start believing in *feng shui* when they try it out . . .

"After the 1984 recession many rich people turned to poor and vice versa. People started asking why and they start hunting for astrologers and geomancers to rectify it. The thing is that 1984 was a time of big change, it is the beginning of a new 60 year series, a new era, so many changes happened then, rich to poor, poor to rich . . .

"I believe that if you are good at *feng shui* people will come to you. Everyone has a mandate in this world, I prefer that people just walk in and find me themselves. This is not an easy line. People can think you are god and will save them. You have to be a good counsellor. They can be so downhearted yet I will see a great opportunity and I will motivate them. This is inside them. It has nothing to do with *feng shui*. You can live in a great house and be lonely. People must find peace and comfort in themselves. People want power and money but this won't make people happy, often they will have enemies."

"The first thing people ask me about *feng shui* is always 'How much will it cost?' At this moment most Singaporeans have a basic knowledge of *feng shui* so it's not too difficult to convince them that *feng shui* is important. So what they really want to know is how much it will cost and what is the job package. If I quote $500 what will it include and how many times I will come. People don't ask 'Does it work'. Do you ever ask your doctor 'Does medicine work?' It is more what can you provide . . .

"Next most common is 'Can the master use the master bedroom?' They are very worried that they are not allowed to use the master bedroom. Some have to use another bedroom and this worries clients. But really 80% of the time the master bedroom is okay...

"Another question is 'How long does it take for the *feng shui* to work?' My answer is not more than six months. If it takes more than six months that means you are very bad or the premises are very bad. There are cases where it works almost instantly, good things happen right away. One of my clients, after I had done his office and his house he called up and asked how come all his staff began to resign. Not all but most of his staff resigned. I told him not to worry because when the *feng shui* works they were in the way and it will throw away all the useless baggage. They might be there working for you five years, ten years but they haven't put in the effort working for you. So it will throw out the bad staff and bring in good staff. He got new staff after that and they were all hard workers, no arguments, no politics, nothing. Also people can expect to have lottery strikes. People's luck improves generally. Sometimes they will strike a lottery on Saturday and then again on Sunday with the same number. Even to me this is amazing...

"The most important thing is that the clients themselves are satisfied with what they want. If what the client wants is a good job then after the *feng shui* is done he is much more likely to find it...

"Say I charge $2,500 to do a $300,000 terrace house. The client says it is expensive but I say it is actually nothing, not even one percent, and I can guarantee you no problems will come. Even a doctor cannot guarantee you that you will have no illness. I can guarantee you that nothing funny will happen. I cannot guarantee that you will have no flu, no fever, that is beyond the point...

"People ask 'When will I get rich after I have consulted you?' They are serious about it though they put it as a joke. There are geomancers that use the advertisement '*feng shui* for health and wealth', so that is the kind of philosophy people have, the kind of expectations. They don't realise that geomancy is an environmental science. It makes sure you do the right thing in the right place at the right time. This is most important. There is no guarantee that they will be rich but everything will be good. That's what I will say. Because we don't know the character of this person. He might be a crook. This is a very important factor. Also opportunity is more important than money that comes straight away. After I fixed a client's beauty salon she was made official beautician for the Miss Universe competition. This kind of promotion will bring her more in the long run than the immediate money. People are wrong to think *feng shui* is an instant money maker."

"There are no surveys and no statistics on how much *feng shui* is used in Singapore but I'm sure it's increasing. It's not used much for locating buildings though. Last year, I had a few special consultancy jobs: three high-rise buildings worth over 200 million dollars each. I had to advise on the site and the design, look through the architectural plans. I also looked at a couple of housing estates and a club with hundreds of members. None of these were government developments and there was never any question about whether to build on the site but how to build on the site. . .

"There are so many important aspects of the surroundings you can't name them all. You have to walk around the site and look at every element surrounding it. You have to check every element that might be good or no good for the site, study the site thoroughly. After you know the site very well, you make a summary of it and you work out where you should enter the site, which side should be the front. Of course there are rules but there are so many rules that there is no simple application. You have to balance the different influences against each other. There is a degree of intuition but it is a lot to do with experience and knowledge. You can't solve these sorts of problems from a book . . .

"The influence of the natural landscape is very great but the client has already bought the site so you have to make the best use of it. There are always bad sites. Some are very bad. It is up to the skill of the geomancer, and if he has no sense of design it will be much more difficult to get the best use of the site. With an architectural background and a good sense of design it is much easier to come up with solutions which are the best in terms of architecture, landscape and *feng shui* all at once . . .

"I heard about *feng shui* during my childhood and thought it was nonsense. I was Chinese educated for some years. I loved Chinese and was interested in the literature. I learned classical Chinese and loved the language but I put it aside when I began doing architecture and didn't use it for many years. I started to pay attention to Chinese things again in 1976. I did brush painting and wrote a book on *feng shui* at the request of a colleague. You can't practise *feng shui* without gaining more and more knowledge about all aspects of Chinese culture. So now I have a list of books on Chinese things. They are all associated: colour, shape, numbers, all symbols. They all have meaning and are interconnected. Learning these things really enriched my life in very tangible ways. There is so much involved, everything that is natural, the forces, landscape, materials. *Feng shui* covers a very wide area . . .

"*Feng shui* is an art of placement so everything we do, however we place things, must be in harmony with the natural landscape. It is about how to do the right thing in the right place at the right time. Anyone who is interested in the environment and nature, *feng shui* will help them live in harmony with everything around them. It is difficult to achieve in a built up environment but geomancers will come up with something that is more comfortable than it otherwise would be."

"Singaporeans are from many countries: China, Asia, Europe. We hardly know about the original Singaporeans. We have five different skin colours and all religions. These are like five different elements. If we only had two colours they would fight, instead we have harmony . . .

"The Chinese previously listened to *feng shui*, it is already five thousand years old. Many of the people who come to Singapore are escaping from fighting, they had no choice and they don't know how to practice *feng shui*. Year by year the Europeans have come in and the economy has been built up. Singaporeans learn English and try to achieve a Western lifestyle and they become financially successful. Then the Europeans got interested in Eastern culture and *feng shui*. This mixture of Eastern and Western values creates harmony. Westerners are concerned with the material, Easterners are more spiritual and family-orientated. Now there is regeneration of Eastern values. People are remembering and returning to Chinese culture. This can happen because of prosperity and education . . .

"*Feng shui* is so important. Years ago there was a sea wall in Singapore and everyone got rich fast because it was holding the wealth in. Then the sea wall was taken down and now all the children go overseas to study and don't want to come back. The MRT is a new dragon. In 1985 the economy was going down very fast. Some people said that the digging underground for the MRT was hurting the *feng shui*, but the MRT is very successful. Soon we had three lines and the economy started to boom. First Japan, then Hong Kong, then Singapore put in MRT systems and after each the economy boomed. The MRT is a dragon, it moves enormous amounts of *qi* ...

"In many other countries trees are being cut down too fast. Trees balance the weather so now even this is being disrupted. Singapore is called the Lion City and the lion is the King of the forest. This is also the garden city. It is full of trees so it can be cool and comfortable. That is why it is important that we keep our trees in Singapore, so the lion can rule comfortably in a beautiful country."

"I have created my own theory because I have had wide experience and read many books, I talk from experience. Geomancy and healing, creation, the universe are all interconnected. I meditated for four hours a night for two years and I started to see the forces of the universe. When you do meditation you don't need the senses. The mind is tuned so fine that you can see the forces moving inside the body. By doing *qi gong* you can increase these forces in your body. The forces are absolutely fundamental to the functioning of humanity and all the universe. Like a computer's function is dependant on electricity, the material components themselves cannot make a computer work. What gives the computer life is the electric force. You can call the force god or whatever you want, but there is one force in the body which controls movement and the proper functioning of every part. It is the same force in the body as in the land ...

"People don't realise that they are infinitely small compared to the force that moves the universe, the planets, the earth, the oceans etc. We are so small we cannot even push a cart ourselves and we think we are so great because we have a mind, we think we can move forces. We can move cars, we can move ourselves, but we can't move mountains, rain, earth. We can't move the tidal wave. We are very small. It is very bad to think we are big . . .

"Now look at the day you were born. Because you were born you will die. This is the positive and negative of life. In between there is sickness, how do you get out of that? The way you do things is to realise that there is death down there and you must realise that what happens in between is not that important except as the interaction of forces. Sometimes you are happy, sometimes you are sad, sometimes you are in love, sometimes you are out of love, sometimes you are very rich, sometimes you are very poor. Whether you are happy or whatever depends on the mind. The mind can heal everything. To me the mind is the most powerful, not the brain: the mind which is connected with the heart, the emotions, is the only medium that can connect us to the force which is running us all the time. If the mind is still and properly trained we become the director rather than the directed. You see the current down there and you say – I will not go into that current because it is not a good current, I will move into this one. You can see whereas the rest are blind to this force. This is merging with god, you are part of the creator not the created . . .

"All material things are a condensation of forces. Running water, electricity, people all have a force field that they create around themselves. The light painted around the saints in both East and West is because the light can be seen – artists are very sensitive people. Everything on earth radiates an energy field which interacts with all other energy fields. There is actually only one energy, call it god or whatever. Behind it is pure joy and tremendous power. . .

"Any place that produces life, trees, there is energy. It is that simple, you just observe the natural environment. If trees grow nicely and there are animals then there is harmony. Nature and the environment is distilled from the five elements. There are minerals, wood, fire, earth and water. Earth is first, minerals are secondary but each and every one either compliments or repels the others . . .

"Pollution is an overabundance of one element. If there is too much water the land will subside. Overabundance of certain things produced by humans or deposited in the wrong place results in the elements being out of balance. These are sick places we live in and so we get sick. In nature all these things would be recycled and balanced...

"The influence of the colours and lighting affects the mind and the well-being of the person. With the person in tip top condition and with the alignment of forces, colours and lighting in harmony, the person will accumulate a lot of energy and be able to do his work well and be happy, because the health and the mind are interrelated. If you are in pain you will never be able to think properly. If a person is in perfect condition the *chakras*[3] are all perfectly charged . . .

"I would rather align people than the building but even better is to align the mind. At a certain point you don't need *feng shui*. Once you get to understand the emotions etc you don't cause as much conflict. Geomancers and doctors can activate the mind by talking to patients but some don't want to get well – so don't treat them, it is a waste of time. Some people really want to be sick. It is their mind making them sick..."

The Geomancers' Businesses

There is a lot of variation in the way that *feng shui* is practised by geomancers and how they organise their businesses. *Feng shui* is very closely related to other classical Chinese disciplines such as astrology, numerology, face reading and name analysis. Astrological analysis is an intrinsic part of *feng shui* in Singapore and all of the geomancers practise a mixture of these arts.

For most of the geomancers, *feng shui* is a full-time occupation, though for others the emphasis of the practice is split between geomantic and more purely astrological services. Three of the geomancers, including one who is very prominent and influential, consult part-time as geomancers while working in other jobs. Most operate on their own, but some have a small staff, usually consisting of an apprentice/assistant geomancer or a secretary or both. One geomancer has seven staff members including draughters, designers and administrators. He claims to have the largest geomantic business in the world and estimates that he deals with a hundred clients

---

[3] An Indian concept of energy centres in the body.

a month on average. This is very unusual, perhaps an example of a new form of big business geomancy. On average, the other geomancers saw about eleven clients each per month.

All the geomancers perceive an increase in the popularity of *feng shui* in Singapore. Some feel that this trend has been occurring for two to five years, others consider that it has been going on for ten years or so. Generally they feel that there are a number of factors acting together to influence this trend. The most important factors are increased prosperity, higher educational levels in the community (which has resulted in a resurgence of interest in Chinese traditions), increased contact with people and businesses in Hong Kong and media attention to *feng shui*. Others also think public interest is being generated by geomancers actively publicising their ideas and services.

People consult geomancers about both their businesses and their homes and, though most geomancers consider the *feng shui* of the home to be more influential than that of the work place, the more prestigious and lucrative geomantic work seems to be in the commercial sector. The more prominent a geomancer is, the more work he or she is likely to do on business premises. Some of these cases are multi-million dollar commercial developments. International banking corporations, large hotel and retail chains and property developers are among these geomancers' clients. Overall, however, about half the work done by the geomancers in this study was in homes and half in commercial properties.

In most cases (about three out of four), clients ask geomancers to examine premises which they already occupied. These consultations are usually prompted by some kind of problem the client is having which he or she thinks might be the result of poor *feng shui*. The geomancer examines the area the client occupies and its surroundings and usually recommends how to improve the situation by moving furniture and fixtures and, occasionally, may advise the client to make some structural changes such as shifting the position of the front door.

In almost all the remaining cases (the other one in four on average), the client has already chosen the premises but the geomancer is brought in before the client moves in. In these cases the geomancer again examines the premises and recommends how the space should be organised to make the very best of the situation. In the case of business offices this will even include the positioning of partitions, sizes and locations of offices for key personnel and organisation of the entrance way and reception area, as well as the usual furniture placement. Sometimes the geomancer's advice will be given to a contracted interior designer to carry out.

In less than three percent of all cases a geomancer is engaged to locate or choose the right place to be occupied by the client. Traditionally this function (the location of auspicious sites) was considered the most important part of geomantic practice. In a densely developed urban environment, where choices are already very limited, obviously this aspect of *feng shui* has to suffer. However, there are also other reasons why *feng shui* is rarely used to choose sites in Singapore as we will see in Chapter 5. The result of this is that the methods of adapting non-ideal sites and making them usable have become the most dominant feature of *feng shui* practice in Singapore.

Another way that *feng shui* in Singapore differs from the more traditional practices found in places like China and Korea is in relation to burials. Grave or burial *feng shui* constitutes an almost insignificant part of the discipline in Singapore. Very few geomancers advise on the geomantic characteristics of burial sites or are engaged to choose them. Three geomancers said that they would occasionally be approached by clients to choose places in the public cemeteries for putting ashes. One of these said that about once a year he would be asked by a client to choose an auspicious burial site, design the tomb and oversee the burial rites. Sometimes this geomancer also performs ceremonies for scattering ashes at sea. He considers the rarity of such work to be a result of both a relative lack of choice about where and how people can be buried in Singapore and the enormous expense involved in this lengthy and labour-intensive process.

In some of the older cemeteries, such as Bukit Timah, there are clusters of very old tombstones that were constructed according to traditional geomantic designs, but many early cemeteries have been destroyed to make way for urban redevelopment. It seems likely that *feng shui* was quite widely taken into account for burials in earlier times and has fallen out of favour due to practical limitations. There is only one Chinese cemetery, at Choa Chu Kang, where corpses can still be buried intact, but this is quite rare. Most people are cremated and the ashes are kept in large cemetery pagodas (**Photo 3**). Geomancers disagree about the relevance of *feng shui* in these situations. Some believe that cremation is not compatible with *feng shui* while others say that the bones or ashes of a person must be in or on the ground for *feng shui* to have any effect.

In fact, Singaporean geomancers disagree about the importance of burial *feng shui* altogether. Whether the burial place of one's earliest ancestors or one's latest is most important is the subject of much discussion. I suspect that this disagreement and the divergence from tradition are the result of changes to burial practices brought about by government regulation. This situation has challenged past theories but it is too early yet for agreement on a new approach to have emerged.

Clearly *feng shui* has regained a strong foothold in Singapore in recent years, though there are still some limitations and differences from classical approaches. Many geomantic businesses are thriving and both commercial and domestic clients regularly seek them out for advice.

In the next chapter, I look at several clients' experiences in detail, examine the actual process of geomantic analysis and discuss a number of the most common problems and solutions that were found.

3
USING *FENG SHUI* IN THE HOME AND OTHER BUILDINGS

This chapter uses a number of recent case studies to illustrate the way *feng shui* is most commonly applied in Singapore. By far the most common use of *feng shui* in Singapore is to ensure that specific buildings, usually homes or work places, are suitable for the people who occupy them. At least nine out of ten cases dealt with by the geomancers in this study fall into this category. I call this aspect of *feng shui* "site analysis" because it focuses very closely on the small chunks of the environment that the client is able to control, usually a particular building and its immediate surroundings.

Inherent Features and Relative Features

To analyse the qualities and faults of a person's home or work place, a geomancer will carefully analyse the intrinsic characteristics of the site such as the structure of the building and the positions of surrounding drains, buildings, intersections and other landscape features. These are the inherent features. As well as that, the geomancer analyses the way the site will interact with the particular occupant. These aspects constitute the relative features. The relationship between a person and a site is usually based on the person's elements: the mixture of earth, wind, fire, metal and water that is considered to be present in each individual, and also in his or her ruling hexagram. These are both considered to express the fundamental makeup of the person and guide his or her relationship with the universe in the most profound manner. Fundamentally, a person's elements and hexagram are both derived from his or her time and date of birth.

Using the *feng shui* compass, the geomancer will examine the compatibility of the occupant and the site. Are the major features of the building in auspicious positions for the occupant? What are the richest and poorest areas of the site? The compass indicates the elemental associations of the cardinal directions, from which the compatibility of the features of the site and the occupant's elements can be determined.

If there are aspects of the site which are intrinsically negative, or there are conflicting elements between the site and the occupier, the geomancer will usually make recommendations intended to remove the conflict or overcome its effect. On occasion the geomancer might consider the situation to be so bad that the client will be advised to move premises. In Singapore, however, geomancers seem extremely wary of making such recommendations, or at least of negative client reaction to them, and so the emphasis is on making the best of the given site for the given user.

Case One

Mr A decided to lease a food stall at the Marina South Hawker Centre[1]. He sought the advice of a geomancer regarding the choice of a specific stall site. Though Mr A had already decided on the location, the geomancer confirmed that, in general, the location of the Hawker Centre was excellent because the shape of the Marina South area resembles a bull's head and horns. Such a natural symbol of strength and endurance is considered very auspicious.

The geomancer examined the various stall sites available within the centre and discovered that all the sites were orientated in the same direction and had the same basic layout. Consequently, in terms of directions and elements all the sites were considered to be the same and fortunately were compatible with Mr A's elements.

The major difference between the various stalls lay in their position in relation to a number of tall straight objects, mainly trees and lampposts, found throughout the complex. An object directly in front of a building, particularly if it is in line with the main door, can obstruct the flow of *sheng qi* to the site and therefore can be very inauspicious. The geomancer carefully selected a stall site which was free from obstruction. A few further faults needed to be overcome however. In all the stalls the front and back doors were directly in line, which is considered detrimental in *feng shui* as *sha qi* travels very easily in straight lines. To obstruct this flow of negative energy the geomancer recommended that Mr A's largest refrigerator be placed in between the doors as a barrier (**Fig. 6**). Also, a door within the stall had been painted green which was considered to be incompatible with Mr A's elements and so he was told to either cover the door or repaint it.

---

[1] Hawker centres are outdoor fast food complexes usually comprising a large number of stalls producing many different types of food and a large area for tables and chairs.

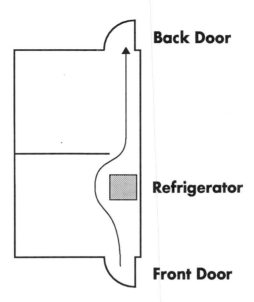

Fig. 6. Floor plan of a food stall with the refrigerator placed between the front and back doors to obstruct sha qi.

When Mr A opened the stall business levels were very low and he seemed to be losing money. He called the geomancer back to re-examine the premises and the geomancer found that Mr A had forgotten to cover the green door. After the colour was changed, business improved dramatically and soon the stall was bringing in a good profit.

Mr A's case illustrates the two different types of features that are significant in geomantic analysis: those which are inherently positive or negative (such as the trees or poles being in line with the front and back doors) and those which are good or bad only in relation to the elements of the particular occupier (the orientation of the stall and the use of the colour green).

In Singapore, the "site" will almost always be a unit of commercial or residential accommodation which the person occupies or is planning to move into. The process of site analysis is the same whether or not the person already occupies the site except, of course, that changes to the premises are more easily made before it is built or occupied than once it is in use.

Case Two

The most well-known Singaporean case involving the renovation of a building subsequent to geomantic analysis is that of the Hyatt Hotel. In a television interview conducted in 1986, the then Manager of the Hyatt stated that prior to the refurbishment, business levels for the hotel were very low. The management consulted, he said, "with a *feng shui* Monk" (who has never been officially named but is generally believed to be Rev. Hong Chun) who made extensive recommendations which were implemented very quickly. Immediately on completion an international airliner was delayed and the hotel was asked if it could accommodate 380 stranded passengers that night. The hotel was full for the next four nights and business levels have been significantly higher ever since.[2]

The renovations are reported in detail by Dr Evelyn Lip in her book *Chinese Geomancy: A Layman's Guide to Feng Shui*[3]. They included a change to the angle of the main entrance doors which was intended to stop evil influences entering the building, moving the fountains in front of the building and replacing them with flower beds and the placement of a flag pole on the fourth floor.

It is commonly believed that a number of other hotels have been renovated on the advice of geomancers, which may be a result of the publicity associated with the Hyatt case. Among the hotels rumoured to have had geomantic renovations are the Shangri-La, the Marco Polo and the Dynasty. Representatives of these hotels, as well as Raffles and the Mandarin hotels which were undergoing renovation at the time of this study, all stated that geomancers had never been engaged to examine these hotels. None of this can really be considered conclusive either way. There can be some reluctance among Singaporeans to be seen to be using geomancy, and so it is possible that these representatives would not know or would not say if in fact geomantic advice had been sought.

An excellent example of a geomancer advising on the design of a site prior to occupation is the case of the Bank of Boston, then in Collyer Quay. This case is not well known or documented. It was investigated through discussions with the geomancer and the interior designer but primarily through information given readily by the personnel of the Bank of Boston.

---

[2] Mr Michael Gray, Manager Hyatt Hotel, "Life and Times", SBC TV, 1986.
[3] Lip, 1979.

Case Three

While in their previous accommodation, the Bank of Boston sought the advice of a geomancer because of business stagnation. After some minor adjustments, business levels were perceived to rise over a period of a year. Later, the bank planned to move to a new building and when a few floors became available in the Tung Centre, Collyer Quay, the same geomancer was engaged to examine the premises.

The geomancer advised that the bank should locate its offices on the 16th floor (16 is an auspicious number) and several recommendations were made regarding the floor plan. The angle of the main door and all the furniture in the reception area was carefully aligned at an angle considered auspicious. The angles of the doors into the managers' offices and the positions of their desks were also carefully arranged. These angles were set in relation to an island which dominates the view from all the offices on the seaward side of the building and is considered to be a strong source of *sheng qi*.

Being a vital source of revenue to the bank, the dealing room was given much attention. It was situated on the side of the building overlooking the harbour and islands which were considered a strong source of *sheng qi*. It was considered very important to locate the dealing room on this side of the building as on the opposite side the view was of the OUB building which has a very dramatic sharp corner pointing towards the Tung Centre. Sharp corners are considered a source of *sha qi* and this one is so strong it could have a devastating effect on anything it pointed at. An island in view of the dealing room also forms a corner, due to reclamation, though this corner is not nearly as sharp or intrusive as that of the OUB Building. To deflect this *sha qi* a statuette of the animal symbol corresponding with the current year of the Chinese horoscope and a vase of fresh flowers are kept in the area of the office which is considered to be directly in line with this current of *sha qi* (**Photo 4**). The position of the main dealing desk was set according to an auspicious angle to the islands which resulted in the dealing room being larger than necessary.

When the bank first moved into the premises it was losing considerable sums of money. The geomancer was called back in and found that a marble design which had not been in the plans had been placed in the lift foyer immediately outside the main doors to the bank. The geomancer felt that its design resembled an old Chinese coin (**Photo 5**), that this symbolised y outside the bank and as a consequence money was being drawn away from the bank. To counteract this negative effect three large pots of ink were placed in the dealing room and a ceremony was performed. Each pot of ink contains a mixture of 12 packets of salt, six bottles of ink and six coins. They each have to be kept filled to overflowing so that crystals form on the outside of the pots (**Photo 6**). These crystals are supposed to capture the tension in the room. Once a pot is covered in crystals the solution is replaced. Bank staff believe that the bank was in complete recovery within 24 hours of the remedies being instituted.

Common Geomantic Problems and Solutions

Arrangement of Furniture and Fixtures

The most common method employed for the arrangement of sites on geomantic principles in Singapore is the careful arrangement of furniture. In the vast majority of cases, geomancers make recommendations regarding the placement of furniture and appliances. The most common furniture items to be the subject of geomantic advice are the master bed, cooking stove and any writing desks.

Case Four
Mr B lives in a Housing Development Board apartment in the Ang Mo Kio area of Singapore. He moved into the apartment late in 1987 with his wife. In 1988 and 1989 he lost two consecutive jobs through redundancy during a time when the economy was generally buoyant. In 1989 Mr B was unable to find another job.

Mr B thought that the geomantic character of the new apartment could be the cause of these problems and he engaged a geomancer. In his analysis of the apartment, the geomancer found a number of inauspicious features which had to be rectified. The stove and sink were opposite each other, which caused a conflict between the elements of fire and water. The ancestral altar was in a heavily trafficked area which subjected it to disturbed *qi*. The dimensions of the altar and a desk were considered to be inauspicious while the bedroom furniture was all at inauspicious angles.

The geomancer advised that the stove be moved out of alignment with the sink. Because the existing stove was built in, it was abandoned and a new stove was bought and located in the recommended position. The ancestral altar was shifted into a still area in the study, and it and the desk were made taller to conform with geomantically auspicious dimensions. The bed, wardrobe and desk were moved to face auspicious directions according to Mr B's elements. Auspicious dates were selected for the rearrangement of these features to take place.

Mr B's dominant element is earth, which is associated with the colour yellow. To introduce more influence of the earth element into his environment, Mr B was advised to paint his front door yellow and incorporate yellow clothes into his wardrobe. The geomancer also advised on what areas of Singapore would be auspicious for Mr B to seek a job in. Within four months he obtained a job in an American airfreight company and had a small lottery win. He believes that these events are a result of the changes to his home. He also states that he feels more at ease in his apartment than before the changes were made.

In Mr B's case much of the household furniture was moved to positions and angles compatible with his elements. The master bed is of prime importance as it is where much of a person's time at home is spent. It must be subject to rejuvenating *qi*. Similarly, the managers' desks are extremely important in an office situation, as in the Bank of Boston case.

In many cases cookers are moved to avoid the fire-water conflict apparent when a cooker is directly opposite a sink or toilet (even through a door or wall). Some geomancers believe, however, that the sink and cooker must be in line of sight through the door for a conflict to exist.

Structural Changes

Generally, geomancers are reluctant to recommend structural changes because of the effort and expense involved and, in most cases, sufficient change can be made internally to avoid such radical action. Structural change is sometimes considered unavoidable to remedy very dire influences. One geomancer, however, never recommends structural changes because he considers the structure of a building to be its bones, which should not be altered. If negative influences can not be overcome in other ways, this geomancer will recommend that his clients move to other accommodation.

In most instances, the position of the main door is considered to be the single most important feature of a site. It is the entrance for *qi* as well as people and the quality of the *qi* is considered to be dependant on the direction it comes from. This has been an element in *Cases One, Two* and *Three*. In some cases, the position of the main door to a building will be physically altered.

Case Five
Mr C is a principal of an international interior design firm with a high profile in Singapore. In his work throughout the region he has come into contact with *feng shui* on numerous occasions.

Suddenly in one year, several employees fell ill, some quite seriously. One staff member had a major operation and one nearly died. When the staff began to talk about possible geomantic problems, Mr C decided to call in a geomancer "to appease them". He contacted a geomancer and told him that he wanted a review of the office. Having an interest in *feng shui* and seeing an opportunity to test it, he deliberately did not tell the geomancer that illness was the reason.

When the geomancer began to examine the premises, he very quickly went to Mr C and told him that regardless of any other minor alterations that may be needed, it was essential that the direction of the main entrance be altered. The geomancer stated that it formed the hexagram called "Illness" and asked if any of the staff had been sick.

The geomancer also recommended that certain desks be orientated toward the south-west and that the colour scheme of the office be completely changed. The reception and lobby, originally a dark green, were painted white, Mr C's office was painted a pale ice blue and the draughting room, previously a bright red, was changed to blue. Initially, Mr C had reservations about all the changes based on his judgments as an interior designer. All of the recommended changes were undertaken, however, and Mr C found that the new colour schemes "felt much better".

Mr C described the changes to the main entrance as "incredibly expensive, difficult and bizarre looking". They involved demolishing the door, ceiling, light fittings and marble floor in the area and importing extra stone and carpet from the U.S.A. As soon as the changes were made two senior staff members, who had been with the firm for twelve years, left. Mr C stated that although they were good staff members he had always felt that they were sources of conflict in the office. He stated that the physical changes seemed to prompt a lot of other changes and within two weeks all sources of conflict in the office had been resolved.

As we have seen in a number of cases colour schemes are very important in *feng shui*. The compatibility of colours with a certain person is determined by that person's elemental makeup up according to their date and time of birth. The original colour scheme conflicted with Mr C's elements but corresponded with the elements of the two staff members who subsequently left. When the colour scheme was changed to suit Mr C's elements it would have become incompatible for the two staff members who were then prompted to leave. The new colour scheme served to harmonise the elemental forces in the office.

In the above case, the alteration of the direction of the door was based on analysis of the hexagrams. The element associated with the direction of the main door is also an important consideration and this should be compatible with the elements of the primary occupant of the site. It is also considered very inauspicious to have the gate to a property and its main door in line, and this will also prompt geomancers to recommend changing the position of the doorway.

Case Six
Mr D, a businessman who lives in the East Coast area of Singapore, moved into a new house in 1987. Soon after moving in he began to experience problems with one of his major contracts at work. Over a period of two years the problem compounded to the point where he was in fear of losing the business. In 1989, he sought advice regarding the geomantic character of the house, which he believed could be the source of the problem.

The geomancer found that the house was generally acceptable with some quite auspicious features. However, the front door was directly in line with the main gate to the property. This was considered to be a source of considerable *sha qi* and very inauspicious. The existing front door was bricked in and a new one was made at the other end of the front wall of the house, out of alignment with the gate.

Since the renovations, the contractual problem has been resolved and Mr D has had a small lottery win. He believes that these events are direct results of the improved geomantic qualities of the house.

Dimensions

Dimensions are also an important part of site analysis. Certain lengths and distances are considered auspicious and others inauspicious, based on the use of the *feng shui* ruler. The dimensions of furniture, doorways and rooms are those most commonly analysed by geomancers. One geomancer had advised a beautician on the *feng shui* of her shop. One of his recommendations was to use a cash box of auspicious dimensions. A chocolate box was selected. As well as having auspicious dimensions, it was not very large and would often be over-full with money. This was considered to be positive because it symbolises an over-abundance of money and flowing into the business. In *Case Seven* (**pp. 47**), structural changes to the internal doors of a house were carried out so that they would be of auspicious dimensions.

Living Things as Geomantic Objects

In some instances geomancers recommend that their clients place living objects in specified positions in their premises. These objects will usually be plants or fish tanks. Fish tanks are considered to encourage prosperity as water and goldfish symbolise wealth.

Plants can be used to symbolise a valued characteristic or object, to correct an imbalance of the five elements by introducing one of them into the environment or to deflect negative influences. Bougainvillea is said to symbolise money and one geomancer believes that this is why it is extremely popular in Singapore. Another geomancer recommended that a client place a potted conifer in his office, as there was a deficiency in the element metal and conifers are rich in that element. Planting conifers on either side of the front gate to a property is also a method of deflecting *sha qi*.

The Role of *Qi* in Site Analysis

Sources of *Sha Qi*

As we have seen, the accumulation of *sheng qi* is the central concern of *feng shui*. Careful location of premises and their orientation in accordance with the elements of the occupier ensures the availability of *sheng qi*. The deflection of many forms of *sha qi* is another of the primary aims in geomantic site analysis.

Sha qi comes in many forms but, because it is considered to move easily in straight lines, the most common sources of it are drains, canals, paths, escalators and roads. If such a feature points toward the site concerned it will be considered extremely inauspicious. One geomancer believes that if a house is in line with a medium-sized storm water drain, the occupants could get very sick and even die within one year. Power lines that cross a property are also considered to be a source of *sha qi*.

Case Seven
Mr E is the manager of a coffee bar in a Singapore hotel and is in his late 20s. He inherited a house from his family and, when deciding whether to live in it himself or to rent it out, he sought a geomantic evaluation. The house was considered to suit Mr E's elements but was subject to two forms of *sha qi*. Firstly, the gate of the property was directly in line with the gate to the property across the road. Secondly, a large number of electric power lines ran down the driveway above the gate. These two influences directed an enormous amount of *sha qi* towards the house. To counteract this, a pair of lion statues was placed, one on each side of the gate, on top of the gate posts. A pair of conifers was also planted just inside the property, one on each side of the gate. As well as that, the master bedroom was considered to be subject to swirling, disturbed *qi*. The client was advised to use one of the smaller rooms as his bedroom and only use the master bedroom for storage and other unimportant purposes. The dimensions of all doorways in the house were also considered to be inauspicious so every doorway was increased slightly in size.

Obstructions such as poles and large trees in front of houses or offices are also considered to be sources of *sha qi* as in *Case One*.

A geomancer related a case which he considered to be one of the worst situations he had ever encountered due to a strong source of *sha qi*. The front gate, front door and kitchen door of a house were all directly in line with each other. Also in line with these entrances, opposite the house, there was a supporting pillar for an overhead railway line. The geomancer stated that the influence of the pillar was extremely negative, but was made even worse by the placement of a traffic sign next to it. Together the configuration looked like the Chinese character for *xia*, which means "down" (**Fig. 7**). He considered that the family's luck was being "pushed down" by this strong source of *sha qi* which was being directed straight through the house.

48 *Feng Shui* In Singapore

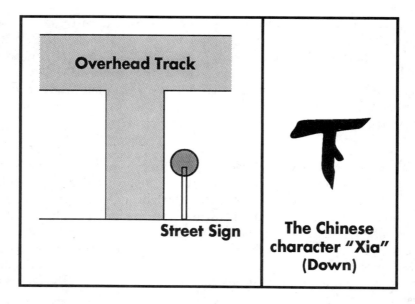

Fig. 7. *Overhead railway track and pillar with street sign forming the Chinese character* **xia**.

The geomancer recommended that a conifer tree be planted on either side of the main gate, and that a pair of small lions be put on pillars on either side of the house, with two larger lions by the front door and two lions on a chest of drawers which faced the front door and were in line with it. He also recommended that the family keep a fish tank on the lucky side of the house and plant many trees outside, on the lucky side of the house, to help their luck grow.

Glare and sharp corners on buildings are also considered to be sources of *sha qi*. The Gateway development is quite controversial because it is clad in reflective glass and has two very acute angles at each end of the complex (**Photo 7**). These are described as "secret arrows" or "black arrows" by geomancers. Most geomancers believed that these characteristics of the Gateway buildings caused financial and labour difficulties and long delays in the completion of the project.

Sha qi can also be generated by human emotions such as anger or fear. One geomancer considered that the negative or aggressive character of criminals could generate negative forces and that only very strong organisations could withstand the influence of a police station nearby as they also generate *sha qi*. Another believed that if extreme suffering occurred in a place, it could be "cursed" with negative emotional energy. Ghosts are also considered to be a form of *sha qi*.

Remedying *Sha Qi*

Sha qi is often deflected or counteracted with the use of geomantic objects such as lion statues. In one wealthy Chinese street in Singapore, about one in four of the houses or shops display geomantic objects used to deflect *sha qi*. In most cases some feature in the environment could explain the use of the object. Some houses had pillars or trees in front of them, and for some the door of the house across the road or their own gate was in line with the front door of the house displaying the geomantic object. Some houses faced a road and a lane at two different "T" junctions, which is considered a very bad situation in *feng shui*, and many of these houses were displaying geomantic objects. In some cases, there were no obvious reasons for the geomantic objects being displayed and in other cases sources of *sha qi* were quite obvious but no remedies were in place.

By far the most common geomantic objects being displayed were mirrors, some with the eight trigrams (*ba gua*) depicted around them (**Photos 8 and 9**). There is some disagreement among geomancers about whether or not such remedies work. Some geomancers believe that mirrors and other talismans are only effective as stop-gap measures and cannot deflect *sha qi* indefinitely. Others believe that they are very effective if used properly. There are two different kinds of trigram mirror, the concave *Ou Jing* for minimising *sha qi* and the convex *Tu Jing* for maximising *sheng qi*. All *ba gua* mirrors use the eight trigrams in the Former Heaven Arrangement which depicts the trigrams in their ideal or heavenly state.

The use of trigram mirrors and other talismans does not necessarily indicate that the advice of a geomancer has been sought. One geomancer felt that many people use trigram mirrors "like Americans use vitamins – just in case" and often they are used incorrectly. Trigram mirrors are so much a part of Chinese tradition and culture that they cannot be considered the sole property of *feng shui* practice. Some aspects of *feng shui* are so ingrained in Chinese culture that they are practised without a clear understanding of their original purpose. The common use of a number of the more aesthetic features of *feng shui*, such as architectural detailings, also suggests that the line between deliberate observance of geomantic practice and less deliberate adoption of Chinese traditions and aesthetics can be unclear.

In a densely developed city where planners have not taken *feng shui* into account, the art of deflecting *sha qi* can be very complex. Most geomancers agree that this and the alignment of furniture in accordance with the forces which suit the primary occupant's elements are the two main features of site analysis.

Ideal Images in Site Analysis

Though it is a relatively small part of site analysis in Singapore, the consideration of ideal and magical images still occurs in the geomantic analysis of people's homes and offices.

The image of the ideal landscape, with mountains at the back, left and right and including lowland or water in front, was used by two geomancers when they described the layout of their offices. Each office is arranged so that the geomancer sits with a solid wall behind. This takes the place of the protective main mountain. Desks or walls to either side form the Azure Dragon and White Tiger and an open area in front of each desk becomes the lowlands of the ideal landscape. At one geomancer's premises an escalator runs parallel to the front wall conducting people to a point at the front-right of the office. The geomancer feels that this has the same effect that a river would by directing people across the front of his shop and thereby creating a source of *sheng qi*. If the escalator pointed directly at the front of his office, however, it would be a source of *sha qi*.

The ideal image of sitting on the side of a mountain overlooking the sea (*zuo shan xiang hai*), which is a variation of the image above, was applied to Mr D's house in *Case Six*. The positioning of the house on its site was said to conform to this image as the site is lower at the front than at the back and the furniture of the split level living room is arranged to look out on the lower front area. A small pool is sited in the ground in the front of the house.

The house has two stories and the same image is applied to the upper landing. A sofa is situated on the upper landing facing the stairwell. A traditional Chinese painting of mountains is hung behind the sofa, while a Western style seascape is on the opposite wall of the stairwell lower down. The two paintings symbolise the mountains and sea in the ideal image. Mr D stated that this was his favourite place in the house and he found it peaceful and invigorating.

Most geomantic images are based on images from nature. This is a way that traditional geomantic appreciations of nature are preserved in the urban environment. In *Case One*, the image attributed to the Marina South area is a bull's head and horns, which is considered very auspicious because it symbolises strength and power. Many other places incorporate images from nature which are considered to influence the occupants.

Case Eight
Mr F is a partner in a Singaporean firm of solicitors. When the firm was planning to take over an extra floor in the building they were already in, Mr F engaged a geomancer to examine the premises. The geomancer advised him to situate the main reception area and the partners' offices on the 16th floor because the number 16 is considered lucky. The geomancer set auspicious dimensions for the partners' offices and advised them to have green carpet on the 16th floor because the word for green and the word for happiness sound the same in Cantonese.

Below Mr F's office, slightly to the right, a building with a revolving restaurant at its top could be seen through a window. The geomancer considered this to symbolise a Mandarin's seal, and so if Mr F sat with this in view it would create the image of a Mandarin's (Imperial Chinese official) chambers. Sitting in this direction Mr F also looked out over the sea, and behind him, through a window to his right he could see a tall building with a convex facade which would constitute a protective mountain for him.

In this case, the ideal image of sitting with a mountain behind while facing the sea is combined with the magical image of the Mandarin's office centred on the Mandarin's seal.

The Bank of Boston offices (*Case Three*) were considered by the geomancer to be in the image of a snail because the building the offices are in uses concentric circles in its design. The geomancer considered that the snail's mouth was located in a particular corner of the office and advised the Bank staff to put up a picture of food there and keep the area clean. Several colour photographs of food are on the wall in this area. This is an example of the image as a functioning system which has been identified in previous studies on *feng shui*. A snail is alive and needs food so, to be complete, the magical image of the snail also needs a component that represents its food.

Wisma Atria is a large department store in Orchard Road. Although he has no direct proof of the matter, a geomancer stated that he believes that the image of the building has been developed around the water element, which probably suits the elements of the owner. The building is clad in translucent blue material and the store logo is a series of stylised waves (**Photo 10**). Waves and the sea are often emphasised in its advertising.

The main entrance to the building is set below street level and customers enter by descending a very wide staircase which curves backward and forward. This resembles a waterfall entering a pool. Consequently, the bottom of the building becomes a reservoir for collecting customers who flow in like water. Water symbolises money and so customers flowing in like water is a particularly auspicious geomantic image. There is also a large aquarium in the bottom floor of the building (**Photo 11**).

Another story involving imagery associated with water was related by a member of the public. Some years ago a building, which was on a site in Raffles Place now occupied by a major shopping centre, was burnt down. Many people were said to have been trapped in the fire and died. Apparently on the advice of a geomancer, the new shopping centre building incorporates a large fountain which forms a waterfall through three stories of the building. This is intended to ease the suffering of the spirits of the people who died in the building and counteract any bad luck resulting from the disaster.

These are merely a few of a large number of geomantic stories associated with buildings in Singapore. The application of *feng shui* to buildings is readily accepted and is quite common. Most Singaporeans only know of *feng shui* as associated with building design and furniture arrangement and many are surprised when they hear it can be applied to the wider landscape.

Photo 1. *Figures of dragons, tigers & birds resting on the roofs of buildings.*

Photo. 2. *Stone statue of a lion-like animal usually placed by the sides of doorways.*

Photo. 3. Cemetery pagoda for ashes.

Photo. 4. Bank of Boston. Statuette of a horse and a vase of fresh flowers to deflect **sha qi**.

Photo. 5. Bank of Boston. A marble design in the lobby resembling an old Chinese coin.

Photo. 6. Bank of Boston. Pots of ink filled to overflowing.

Photo. 7. The Gateway. The reflective glass and sharp corners of its twin buildings are considered to be sources of **sha qi.**

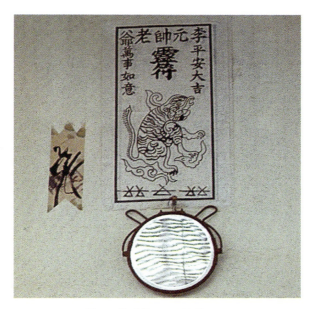

Photo. 8. Mirror and talisman.

*Photo. 9. Mirror with the eight trigrams (**ba gua**).*

Photo. 10. Wisma Atria shopping centre with its store logo.

Photo. 11. Wisma Atria. A large aquarium in the centre of the basement.

Photo. 12. A boat at the Singapore River with eyes painted on its bow.

Photo. 13. The Merlion at the Singapore River.

4
LANDSCAPE AND LOCATION

The landscape analysis methods of the Form School have most often caught the attention of Western commentators on *feng shui*, as this is the most tangible branch of the discipline and is probably most compatible with European thought, particularly with geographic theory. Traditionally, landscape analysis was the starting point, and a very important part, of any geomantic examination of an area. Though in practice it has become less dominant as *feng shui* has been applied more often in heavily built up areas where the natural landscape is less of an influencing factor and choices about location are very limited, it is still a rich source of geomantic information and a vital part of the discipline.

While landscape analysis is primarily used to identify auspicious locations, landscapes are also considered to be alive with nature's energies and many picturesque and powerful images are often developed around particular areas. In the *feng shui* tradition, landscapes may be vested with particular personalities and local people would often consider the nature of their locality to be a guiding force in their lives. In this way, the relationship of people to nature, as shaped by *feng shui*, is very intimate.

Where geomancy has been well established for a long time, the geomantic image applied to any particular area would usually be generally agreed on by local geomancers and well known to the resident population. Though this is not the case in Singapore, geomancers do attribute various interesting images to the most significant landscape features of the island. A range of images is often applied to the same areas and these are almost always the starting points for many ideas about which areas of Singapore are auspicious or inauspicious.

Geomancers tend to analyse the landscape of Singapore at three different scales. They are: the position of the island among its neighboring countries in the region; the island as a whole; and various smaller areas within the island. The landscape at each of these levels can be imbued with geomantic meaning.

The *Feng Shui* of Singapore in Relation to the Region

Within the relationships between Singapore and the various countries in Singapore's vicinity, geomancers saw a fascinating variety of images which are considered to influence the nature and development of the region. Most of the geomancers were extremely enthusiastic about Singapore's physical location, which is particularly auspicious in relation to the Malaysian peninsula and the islands of Indonesia. Though its position was described as being almost ideal by most geomancers, one retired geomancer argued that Hong Kong's location is in fact even better.

The common theme running through the various geomancers' descriptions of the regional landscape which Singapore is a part of is the classical depiction of the ideal landscape.

The traditional images of the main mountain, azure dragon and white tiger are each applied to the landmasses of Singapore, Indonesia and Malaysia in three different ways. In one representation, the island of Sumatra is considered to be the white tiger and Borneo (Kalimantan) is the azure dragon. Flanking Singapore, these two islands are considered to protect it from winds and *sha qi* and act as guardians. The Malaysian peninsula forms Singapore's main mountain and protects it from the north. Open sea lies to the south.

This image corresponds almost exactly with the classical form of the ideal landscape. It is also consistent with the principle of "sitting on a mountain facing the sea". In each of these ways Singapore is an ideal site and could hardly be in a more auspicious position. As it occupies the position of main mountain, mainland Malaysia is considered to be the protector of Singapore's abundant *sheng qi* rather than a recipient of *qi* for itself. One geomancer stated that as a consequence of this Malaysia could never be as prosperous as Singapore which receives most of the *qi* of the region.

Sheltered on both sides by other islands, the weather conditions in Singapore are quite calm and consistent. The geomancers claimed that because of this, the island is protected from hurricanes and typhoons and the sea is almost always calm. This characteristic was considered especially significant not only for the safety and comfort of Singaporeans but because water is a symbol of money and in *feng shui* a view of a calm sea is conducive to the accumulation of wealth. Singapore's growing affluence was attributed to its auspicious geomantic situation.

The second variation of this very ideal interpretation of Singapore's geographic position again incorporates the images of the azure dragon and white tiger (**Fig. 8**). In this case, however, they are fighting over Singapore, which is attributed the image of a pearl. Again Sumatra is the white tiger, but this time the azure dragon is peninsular Malaysia. Being depicted as a pearl indicates that Singapore is in the ideal position in this landscape, although the dragon and tiger forms do not curl around the island in a horseshoe shape. The image of the pearl is a symbol of the energy and richness attributed to the ideal site and, again, is an image associated with Singapore's rapid economic development in recent decades.

Another interesting aspect of this image is that of conflict or competition between Indonesia and Malaysia. A geomancer believed that although the dragon and tiger were in conflict, they would always be competing with each other in order to "win the pearl", and so this would actually be advantageous to Singapore and would ensure its dominance in the region.

The final depiction of Singapore's location in the region differed more from the classical ideal landscape. In this image Singapore is considered to be a pearl which is being spat from the mouth of a fish whose throat is formed by the Malaysian peninsula. Though this may seem quite strange, it is considered to be very auspicious by the geomancer concerned. In its position at the mouth of the whole Asian sub-continent, Singapore embodies all the accumulated energy of South East Asia. The pearl represents this *qi* whereas a piece of food in this position might be devoured by the fish. Again, Singapore's position is considered to symbolise and ensure its prosperity.

The geographical position of Singapore was considered by early European colonists to be extremely advantageous in the region because it was seen to be in an ideal position to become an important trading post and service centre for the whole of South East Asia. Singapore's recent success has also largely been based on the current government's determination to develop these roles as Singapore's economic niche.

Fig. 8. *The azure dragon and the white tiger fighting over the pearl.*

Many of the geomancers said that their geomantic descriptions and the Western geographic and economic interpretations of Singapore's position were very compatible. Though clothed in different language and imagery, *feng shui* and economic geography seem to have arrived at similar conclusions about the advantages of Singapore's place in the world.

Feng Shui Images of the Island as a Whole

Applying images to landscapes at a large scale is very important in *feng shui* and it is clear that Singaporean geomancers have put a lot of thought into the symbolism of the location of their country. Even more important, perhaps, is the geomantic image of the island of Singapore itself. Studies from Korea and other Oriental countries certainly seem to suggest that most important landscapes would be attributed a human or natural image. Surprisingly, there is little agreement among geomancers about the image of the island of Singapore and some are even reluctant to venture an opinion about it. Nevertheless, several geomancers had strong, if sometimes conflicting, opinions on the geomantic image, and therefore nature, of the island as a whole.

Carried over from the analysis of Singapore's position in the region, the image of a pearl was most commonly attributed to the island. The image is more symbolic of the ideal nature of Singapore's regional position, however, than a functioning image from nature. More orthodox natural images were also applied to the island but these varied widely.

Firstly, the image of a crab is attributed to the island (**Fig. 9**). The crab's pincers and legs correspond with the east and west sides of the island and the head and eyes are in the centre of the southern area. This image was not considered to symbolise any national or cultural characteristics by the geomancer who described it.

Similarly, the image of a flying eagle is applied, with its wings on the sides of the island and its head and beak at the bottom (**Fig. 10**). The areas of Singapore which correspond to the joints where the eagle's wings join its body are considered to be very strong, powerful areas and the geomancer who put forward this image felt that these points corresponded with areas of Singapore which were very rich in *sheng qi*. Sentosa Island, immediately to the south of the main island, represents a piece of food for the eagle.

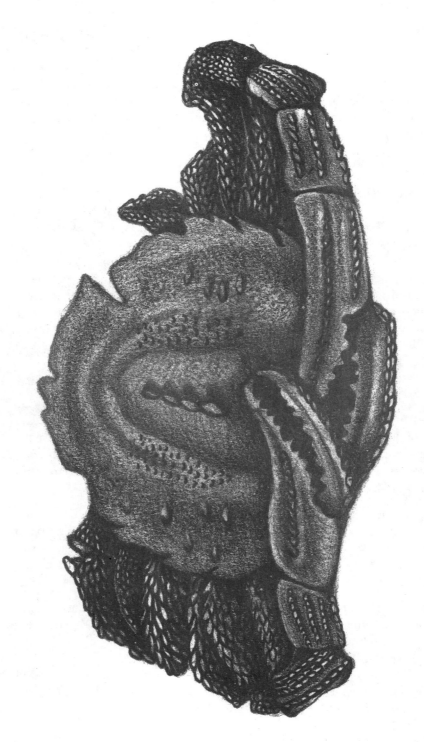

Fig. 9. Singapore in the image of a crab.

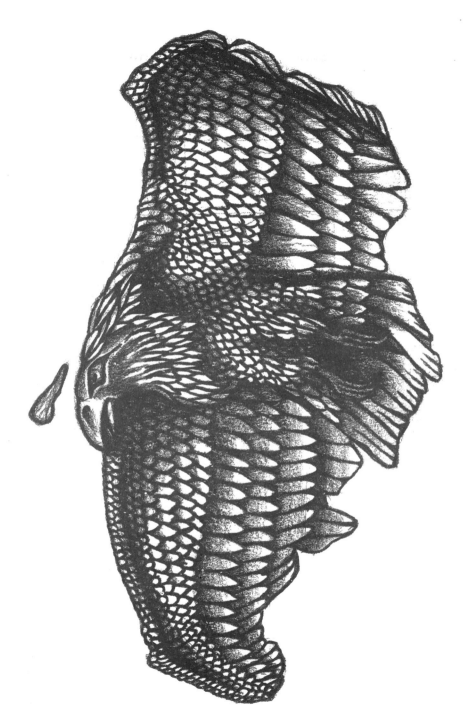

Fig. 10. Singapore in the image of a flying eagle.

This conforms to the traditional requirement that the image has all the components of a functioning system from life: an eagle requires food to survive. The eagle was also considered by the geomancer to represent the nature of Singapore as a nation because like an eagle "Singapore flies high and gets what it wants."

Perhaps one of the most appealing images of the island expressed by a geomancer was that of an old Chinese coin. Ancient Chinese coins were often irregular in shape with a hole in the centre. The geomancer felt that Singapore's irregular lozenge shape and its reservoirs corresponded with this. Commonly, geomantic images of areas are also supposed to represent some characteristic of the people who live there, as we have already seen. In this case the geomancer felt the image to be entirely appropriate as it symbolised Singapore's importance as a financial and trading centre.

Being so important, the image of a city or place which corresponds with the nature or characteristics of the people who live in it could even become an important guide for their behaviour. To disturb the image by changing or destroying one of its features might lead to disaster, so great care would traditionally be taken when any environmental changes were made. Of course, this can only occur where the image is generally agreed on and where there is some co-operation from those in authority. The geomantic tradition in Singapore is not that strong, and so these images do not seem to affect the lives of Singaporeans.

The lack of agreement about the imagery of Singapore is probably symptomatic of its relatively weak geomantic tradition. Most geomancers probably rest their ideas more on their own interpretations and imaginations than on tradition, though it is quite possible that a stronger geomantic tradition is developing. Singapore has been changing very rapidly and continues to do so. As the government strives to create a strong Singaporean identity for its people, geomancers are also trying to create a geomantic identity for the island.

Feng Shui and the Analysis of Areas within Singapore

As with the whole of Singapore, the analysis of smaller areas within it is not as detailed or widely known as could be expected. This is also likely to be attributable to the relatively weak geomantic tradition. Geomancers describe the island in a variety of ways which can be quite different from each other, but there are some aspects which overlap and some very general ideas are widely agreed upon. Geomantic images are associated with many of the most prominent landmarks but there does not appear to be a rich body of geomantic imagery associated with the landscape which is well known or accepted. Again, it is possible that the geomantic tradition of the future is being developed now. It is also possible that some of the ideas now in circulation are related to geomantic beliefs which may have been more prevalent in the 1800s.

The west, south and east coasts of the island are generally considered to be auspicious areas because closeness to the sea can encourage the accumulation of *sheng qi*. The north of the island is not thought to be as good because it is so close to Malaysia and the influence of the water in between is very limited. Also the north of the island is its back and facing north is like facing backwards into the mountain (Malaysia) rather than towards the sea. Traditionally in geomancy, negative influences are said to prevail from the north.

The east coast is generally considered to have better geomantic characteristics than the west because there is more *sheng qi* available from the sea on that side. This coast has important and quite prestigious shopping, commercial and residential areas, while the west coast is more orientated toward the industrial sector and is considered by the geomancers to have been slower to develop. This pattern of development is believed to be a direct result of the geomantic character of the respective areas.

The areas around rivers and reservoirs are also generally considered to be auspicious due to the influence of water. One geomancer discussed the idea that there is a hierarchy of types of water bodies in terms of their beneficial effects. The most beneficial is sea (though it has to be calm to be auspicious), the next are rivers, then reservoirs and lakes, followed by canals, pools, fountains and finally fish tanks and water tanks. This hierarchy seems to suggest that larger and more natural areas of water are most beneficial while smaller, human-made bodies of water are less so. Water which is contaminated, fast-moving or travels for long distances in very straight lines, such as in storm water drains and pipes, is considered very inauspicious to the point where it can be a serious health hazard.

Some geomancers apply the terms "Azure Dragon", "White Tiger" and "Main Mountain" to specific landforms in Singapore to describe the geomantic structure of the island. The Azure Dragon is considered to lie on the east coast, the White Tiger in the west and Bukit Timah is designated the Main Mountain. Bukit Timah itself has been heavily quarried, which many geomancers believe has reduced its auspicious qualities though it is still generally considered to be a very auspicious area. It is one of the most high-class and expensive residential areas in Singapore, dominated by detached bungalow houses with independent grounds.

The southern area of the island is protected by Bukit Timah and faces towards the sea. It is widely believed to be the most auspicious area in the whole of Singapore. The east coast is also thought to be very auspicious because of the strong *yang* force associated with the Azure Dragon.

In contrast, to some geomancers, Azure Dragon and White Tiger refer only to directions and cannot be applied to particular landforms or areas.

Geomancers also call mountains or hills and veins of *qi* that run through the ground "dragons". Most geomancers believe that a number of dragons exist in the landscape of Singapore. Some of these correspond with hills, but in most cases there is very little variation in the landform, though some of this is the effect of quarrying.

The north or north-west is considered to be the place where *qi* enters the island and where the dragons' tails lie. This implies that the source of Singapore's *qi* is in Malaysia or the South East Asian sub-continent. The heads of the dragons are in the south and east of the island which is the destination of the *qi* that flows through them. The dragons are considered to lie mainly on a meandering line that runs roughly from the north or north-west to the south or south-east through the centre of the island. Bukit Timah, Holland Road, and Orchard Road areas all lie on these dragons and the dragons' heads are in the Singapore River area which is the main recipient of *qi* for the island and therefore very auspicious. The affluence and importance of these areas are considered to be a result of the influence of these dragons.

One geomancer has developed a detailed and comprehensive analysis of the geomantic character of the island in which he considers the structure of Singapore to be dominated by five major dragons (**Fig. 11**). His analysis is probably partly based on traditional ideas of Singapore's landscape but also appears to incorporate many ideas of his own. His analysis brings together many of the ideas and approaches of other

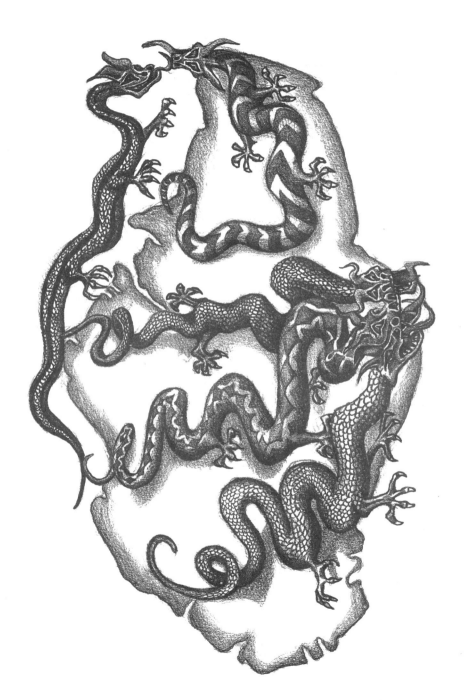

Fig. 11. The island of Singapore dominated by five major dragons.

geomancers too, from which he has developed a theoretical approach that seems systematic and thorough. As an influential and very successful geomancer, his ideas could well have considerable influence on the growing geomantic tradition of Singapore.

The five dragons correspond with the five directions of Chinese tradition: western, central, southern, eastern and northern. The geomancer believes that each of the dragons corresponds to a chain of "mountains" or hills except for the northern dragon which is the Strait of Johor separating the island from the Malaysian peninsula. The central and southern dragons lie close to each other on a north-south axis through the centre of the island and, along with the western dragon, their heads are found in the southern part of the island near the mouth of the Singapore River. The heads of the dragons indicate an abundance of *qi* in this area.

The Singapore River itself is not one of the five primary dragons, but it is considered a lesser dragon and is very important to the success of the area nearby. The river is generally considered to be a very important feature in the geomantic landscape. The mouth of the Singapore River is the point at which much of the *qi* of the island accumulates. This is seen to be the cause for the historical development of the area which, in colonial times, was the seat of government, the port and the hub of trade and marketing. In modern times, the river is considered the source of *sheng qi* for the financial and commercial district immediately to its south. An image commonly given to the last stretch of the river near the financial district is that of a full-bellied carp, which is a symbol of prosperity. There are a number of geomantic stories about the river which reflect its geomantic and historical importance, some of which are discussed below.

The success of a number of developments in various areas is also attributed to the influence of dragons. The position of Changi Airport is considered very auspicious because the head of the eastern dragon is located at that site. The airport's success and continued expansion is believed to be the result of the geomantic quality of the site and the abundance of *sheng qi*. In themselves, the airport and all parts of the transport infrastructure such as motorways and the commuter rail system are generally considered to be human-made dragons as they facilitate movement of people, goods and information and such movement is a type of *qi*.

Geomancers also refer to certain roads as dragons either because they are considered to have developed along the line of a naturally occurring dragon or because they facilitate movement of people and goods and therefore *qi*. Orchard Road and Beach Road are both widely considered to be dragons.

Orchard Road is the main shopping street in Singapore. It is the focus of tourist and up-market local shopping and dining interest and is a centre of activity during some festive seasons. Most of the major hotels are found in this area. Orchard Road is considered to have developed along the path of a dragon in the land and geomancers believe this natural dragon is the source of the area's success. The dragon corresponding with Orchard Road is considered to lie between Tang's department store and the Istana, the President's official residence.

Beach Road lay on the natural sea front until a major reclamation was carried out in the area. Together, Beach Road and East Coast Road constitute a human-made dragon which probably indicates the path of a natural dragon in the landscape. Traditional geomantic images of the ideal landscape are applied to this area. It is described as either two dragons holding a pearl between them or a dragon and a tiger playing with a ball.

The Plaza Hotel is said to stand in the position of the pearl where the cave or ideal site is located. There is a local story that some decades ago a Taiwanese geomancer had identified the auspiciousness of this site but for some time the land was not available for sale. When the site finally came up for sale the current owner had heard of its geomantic value and bought it immediately to build the Plaza Hotel. The geomancer who related this story also considers that the Plaza Hotel is of very auspicious geomantic design containing within itself elements which symbolise mountains and sea.

Of the geomancers who rent accommodation for their *feng shui* practices, a substantial majority have located their offices in the Beach Road/East Coast Road area. While rents are generally cheaper in this area than in Orchard Road, this indicates quite a clear preference over many other areas and seems to demonstrate a consensus about the geomantic qualities of the east coast.

It is not surprising that, whenever possible, geomancers will use their skills to decide where to locate their offices and homes. When one geomancer got married and was eligible to apply for his own apartment from the Housing and Development Board (HDB), he chose not to because he considered his parents' apartment so auspicious. He felt that the site of the apartment constituted an ideal landscape. The apartment faces the Kallang River with a horseshoe-shaped road encircling it behind. Another apartment block between the road and his building forms the Main Mountain, a community centre on the right is the White Tiger and a temple on the left is the Azure Dragon. While the ideal nature of the site was a very important consideration for him, his decision to stay at his parents' apartment was also influenced by the configuration of the apartment itself which suited him in terms of elements and directions.

Within the analyses of the Singaporean landscape offered by the majority of geomancers there are areas of considerable agreement and consistency which seem to correspond with traditional geomantic ideas. Overall, however, this body of analysis is quite superficial and sketchy. Landscape analysis is still considered to be a relatively minor part of *feng shui* in Singapore, probably as a result of the very limited choice people have over where they live in the first place. All of the geomancers addressed the geomantic character of the human landscape (buildings, roads, developments) more readily than that of the natural landscape. This would be considered unusual in traditional circumstances.

Magical Images of the Landscape of Singapore

Generally, geomantic images associated with the land are less abundant in Singapore than would be expected of an Oriental city with a longer or stronger geomantic history. It is quite possible that there was once a richer tradition of these images which has substantially been lost. Much of the traditional imagery is associated with the area in the south of Singapore, near the Singapore River.

The image of the Singapore River as a full-bellied carp is considered very auspicious for the adjacent financial district. The boats of the Singapore River and harbour area also have geomantic associations. In the past, most had eyes depicted on their bows (**Photo 12**). Originally, these eyes were carved in relief and painted onto the sides of the boats, and charms and offerings were made until the eyes were "opened". These imbued the boat with the characteristics and abilities of a live goldfish so that the boat could go into the sea and find its way safely on its voyages. One geomancer said that over time the tradition has dwindled. Gradually the eyes were no longer carved but just painted on the bows of the boats and instead of the original green canopies, brown ones became commonplace. These changes symbolised that the fish were growing old and dying. Now it is uncommon to see eyes on the bows of boats.

Another story refers to Fort Canning Hill, which stands very close to the Singapore River. Its geomantic image is that of a powerful tiger. When the colonial government built a fort on it, the tiger woke up and the *qi* in the area was stimulated so that Singapore could begin to flourish. Later, the National Theatre was built by the hill and this continued the flow of *qi* to the hill even after the Fort was no longer in use. When the National Theatre was demolished, however, the supply of *qi* was stopped and this is said to be a cause for a recession in the mid 1980s. When the MRT was completed and a station placed near the hill, the source of *qi* was reopened to the tiger and Singapore began to flourish again.

It is also believed by many geomancers and other locals that Liang Court, which comprises a block of apartments, hotel and shopping complex built opposite Fort Canning Hill, was built taller than the hill and clad in strong orange coloured tiles to represent another, bigger tiger. This is so that it could counteract the strong *qi* from the tiger of Fort Canning Hill which would otherwise "eat Liang Court up".

One geomancer associates a large number of geomantic images with areas around Singapore but some of these are solely related to the character of the population inhabiting the place or the function of that place rather than the physical landscape of it. This is a somewhat untraditional approach. It appears that due to the recent upsurge of interest in *feng shui* in Singapore, geomancers are currently analysing the landscape and creating images for it. Some of these images may capture the public imagination and become a part of the Singaporean geomantic tradition while others may disappear over time.

According to this geomancer, the image of an elephant and a rhinoceros is attributed to Pierce Reservoir, and the reclaimed area of Marina South is given the image of a dragon's head, both on the basis of the shape of the landscape features. In contrast, Kandang Kerbau Hospital, the major maternity hospital in Singapore, is represented by a mother pig and piglets as an image of fecundity. This is based on the purpose rather than the landscape features of the place.

One stretch of Chinatown which has many clan association houses is represented by a centipede which symbolises the organisations by being "one body supported by many legs".

Bishan is a new town in the north of the island which was constructed over an old cemetery. Many people have reported seeing ghosts in this area and the geomancer also considered it to be a place where many very clever people live, so the area was given the image of monkeys playing. Monkeys are associated with the spirit world in the Chinese tradition and are noted for their cleverness.

It remains to be seen whether these sorts of images, which are not based on any particular similarity to the physical landscape, will take hold and survive in the Singaporean mind. It is not surprising, however, given the practical limitations on locational choice in Singapore, to see geomantic images moving away from their traditional emphasis on landscape.

Limits on the Analysis of Landscape and Location

Through most of Chinese history, landscape and location were the foundation and main focus of geomantic theory and practice. *feng shui* grew in an environment dominated by the landscape, in rural and urban settings where population density was nothing like that of major cities today. People still had wide choices about where they could locate houses and other buildings. The practices of landscape analysis have become devalued in modern Singapore, as they have to a greater or lesser extent in major Chinese cities generally. With the pressure on land experienced in densely populated areas, locational choices are naturally limited.

In addition to this, for at least two decades Singaporeans have had very little choice about where to locate their homes and offices. This is discussed in Chapter Five. It seems logical that in a situation where the public has very little locational choice, the geomantic analysis of landscape and locations will become less important. In Singapore, this appears to have been accommodated to some extent by an unusually heavy emphasis on the methods for adapting given non-ideal sites to given occupiers. Most geomancers consider, however, that the use of *feng shui* to choose sites is very slowly becoming more popular, due possibly to greater affluence, increased knowledge of *feng shui* and a greater degree of choice being given to tenants of the Housing and Development Board.

5
THE GOVERNMENT, THE PUBLIC AND *FENG SHUI*

Undoubtedly, *feng shui* in Singapore is different from both its traditional roots and from other contemporary forms such as the practices found in Hong Kong. In this chapter, I intend to give readers some idea of what makes geomancy in Singapore what it is. I will discuss some of the historical and political influences on Singaporean society which, I feel sure, have had a significant effect on the way *feng shui* manifests itself in this unique environment.

How is *feng shui* in Singapore different from that of other places in which it is practised? Studies have been conducted in China, Hong Kong and Korea. These have generally shown that *feng shui* has an identifiable impact on the cultural landscape, that is on the way that people have modified the natural landscape and created an environment to meet their own needs. Usually, *feng shui* will have had some effect on where buildings and other features of the city, such as cemeteries, have been located. As well as that, certain natural landscape features will have been carefully left alone. In Singapore, these effects are not widely apparent.

Quite a lot of material has been written in English on *feng shui*. Interestingly, Singapore is almost totally absent from this literature. There is plenty of information on *feng shui* practice in Hong Kong, China and Korea, but Singapore is only briefly mentioned in two works. Sarah Rossbach cites an example of the effect of *feng shui* in Singapore, stating that a house at the end of a straight street sold for $10,000 less than its market value because its location was considered inauspicious. Maurice Freedman states that a Housing and Development Board architect told him that front doors of apartments in Singaporean housing estates do not face each other because of geomantic objections from tenants.

On reflection, it is not surprising that Freedman, who wrote prolifically about a range of topics associated with Hong Kong and Singapore, restricted his discussions of *feng shui* almost exclusively to Hong Kong and limited his work on Singapore to the social institutions of the Chinese as a dispossessed, migrant group.

There is very little indigenous Singaporean literature on *feng shui*, though in just the last few years the amount has been growing, particularly that written in Chinese. Of the literature in English, Dr Evelyn Lip, a member of the Architecture Department of the National University of Singapore, has published several books on *feng shui* and related topics such as astrology and temple architecture. Other geomancers have recently begun to publish material on *feng shui*, a small part of which provides geomantic analyses of the Singaporean landscape.

Most other published Singaporean material on *feng shui* focuses on the design aspects of harmonising the elemental make up of an occupant with his or her home or office through careful orientation of furniture and fittings. Very little attention is paid to the role of landforms and the choice of locations in this material. No surveys of Singaporean geomantic behaviour or the impact of *feng shui* on the Singaporean environment have been published previously.

Early Beginnings

Soon after Sir Stamford Raffles acquired Singapore by treaty on 6 February 1819, he decided on a layout for the town, designating areas for the business sector and for the Chinese, Indian, Arab and European populations. This basic scheme continued into the 1970s and is still in evidence today. Thus, one of the most influential arrangements of the island city in its modern history was carried out by its original European colonist. There is no record that *feng shui* was taken into account at that stage.

There is some evidence of geomantic practice in the 19th century but most of this is associated with architectural detailings of buildings from that period, some of which still stand today. Chinese culture and influence did not, however, become dominant in Singapore until recent times.

It is well established that active geomantic practice, particularly that associated with the location and design of buildings, is not the domain of the very poor. Early Chinese settlers in Singapore were not only poor but transient and relatively powerless. At the beginning of the 20th century, only ten percent of the Chinese population was born locally and only 20 percent of the Chinese population was female. At this time, success in Singapore was dependant on a degree of absorption into Malay culture. Although by 1947 Chinese constituted 80 percent of the population, they were still a political minority until the 1960s. Even Chinese kinship ties were considered to be relatively weak in Singapore as late as the 1970s[1].

As Chinese cultural practices, particularly those associated with kinship, are so fundamental to the traditional practice of *feng shui*, it is not surprising that the discipline has only begun to take hold in a more formal and active way in the recent past. It seems likely that recent prosperity has allowed an increase in the popularity of geomantic practice. Also, strong Chinese influence has been established through the government in the last 20 years and a resurgence of interest in Chinese culture is very apparent.

Feng Shui and Public Planning in Contemporary Singapore

Feng shui is not officially practised or condoned by the government. This is not unusual in itself in contemporary Oriental cities, but combined with the rigorous regulation of city planning and development in Singapore, this could explain the comparative lack of impact of *feng shui* on the wider scale.

Since independence on the ninth of August 1965, the government of Singapore has embarked on an intensive and highly-planned development programme which has involved the almost total rebuilding of the city and major reorganisations of the population. Consequently, it is now very hard to tell how much *feng shui* influenced the Singaporean landscape in the past. Development of all kinds, and particularly the location of any development, is regulated by the Singaporean government through a "Master Plan".

The major government planning agency is the Urban Redevelopment Authority (URA). The URA administers the Master Plan, which is a long term development plan governing residential, commercial and infrastructural development. This plan is reviewed every five years. Generally when a development is due to take place, a specific site will be released

---

[1] Freedman, 1968.

by the URA for a stated purpose such as entertainment, residential or hotel development.

Representatives of the URA state that the agency does not take *feng shui* into account in any way. Though there is no specific policy against the use or consideration of *feng shui*, it is not among the criteria for choosing sites or redeveloping them.

A URA planner in charge of a large and complex development, which was at the planning stage during this study, believes that a number of *feng shui* principles to do with the principles of sunlight, wind and aspect are a matter of common sense. He stated that these factors are taken into account as a matter of course, though there has not been any active attempt made by the URA to incorporate geomantic features or analysis. Once sites are obtained by developers, however, *feng shui* can be taken into account and there is evidence that this has occurred in some developments.

As the primary determiner of the location of development in Singapore, the URA, by not taking *feng shui* into account in its planning, effectively stops any possibility of *feng shui* influencing the locations of developments and buildings.

The Housing and Development Board (HDB) is in charge of residential development in accordance with the Master Plan. Approximately 80 percent of Singapore's population live in state housing in new towns which have all been located and built since the 1960s.

While location and timing of housing development is controlled by the URA, the HDB is responsible for the internal design of the new towns. As mentioned above, in an article written in 1968, Freedman recorded that a chief architect of the HDB had said that, after complaints from occupants concerned about *feng shui*, front doors of apartments would not face each other in future housing developments.

A representative of the HDB confirmed to me that front doors of units do not face each other in HDB apartment buildings, but she believed that this was done for reasons of privacy. She also related that in earlier designs for the landscaping of new town grounds, earth mounds were sometimes placed around buildings. After some ground floor tenants complained about the earth mounds because of their supposed negative geomantic characteristics, the HDB stopped incorporating them into their designs.

The representative insisted, however, that the change was instituted for the practical purpose of allowing more light into the ground floor areas, not purely because of concern about *feng shui*.

This representative also believed that some younger HDB architects may have been exposed to geomantic theory through Dr Lip's classes at the National University of Singapore and this could affect their designs, but she stated that this could only occur as a result of personal influence, not HDB policy. One geomancer claims that some HDB architects have attended small private classes he has given about *feng shui*. These could be informal sources of geomantic influence in HDB developments.

Until 1990, HDB apartments were allocated to families by the department and the recipients had no choice about which apartments they wished to occupy. Apartments could only be resold after a minimum of five years and the number of times a person could buy or sell apartments was restricted. Again this is evidence that locational choice is very limited.

Apartment owners can renovate their apartments and can make minor structural changes but these must be limited to the internal design of apartments. Clearly, any potential for geomantic influence in housing developments is largely curtailed as a result of HDB policy.

Some of these restrictions now seem to be changing and this could allow *feng shui* to have some influence in HDB developments. Since early 1990, new buyers have been allocated a block of flats and can choose which flat they want within the block on a first come first served basis. Resale is still restricted. Two geomancers stated that within a few months of the change in policy they had each been employed to choose an apartment for a client within an HDB block. As resale pricing has also been deregulated since early 1990, it may in future be possible for values of HDB apartments to reflect geomantic qualities.

The Mass Rapid Transit Corporation (MRT) is another major agency involved in development in Singapore due to its wide power to acquire and develop property for building the MRT system. A number of *feng shui* stories relate to the development of the MRT system. There is also some coincidence between geomantic colours and those used to identify the various MRT lines. The southern line is red and the eastern line is green, which correspond directly with the colours associated with those directions in *feng shui*. The northern line is yellow and the western line is blue. In *feng shui*, yellow is the colour associated with the centre, but is also associated generally with China which, of course, is north of Singapore. Traditionally north and east would be black and white respectively, but this could not easily be the case on a map such as the MRT route map because black and white would usually be used for lettering and background.

Many geomancers also believe that the MRT lines follow the lines of natural dragons in the Singaporean landscape. One stated that he believed the MRT was routed in accordance with the recommendations of the very famous geomancer-monk, Reverend Hong Chun. Of course, this cannot be substantiated in any way and whether or not it is true is less important than the fact that the story has caught the imagination of some members of the public. The MRT system is successful and some Singaporeans will raise *feng shui* as one of the reasons for this.

A representative of the MRT was adamant that any correspondence between geomantic principles and the MRT was pure coincidence. He repeated many times that the MRT was the product of rational planning, not *feng shui*, emphasising that there is a conflict between the two.

Nevertheless, one geomancer claims that he was engaged to advise on aspects of the Marina South MRT station because of a problem which he would not give any details of (on the grounds of client confidentiality). The MRT representative stated that this could be possible because private contractors built each station and they had some control over design which would allow them to take *feng shui* into account, if they chose to do so. He insisted, however, that the MRT Corporation had nothing to do with such an action.

It is likely that there is very little active or conscious geomantic influence in government planning and actions in Singapore. The representatives of the agencies I contacted were concerned that the agencies be seen to be acting "rationally". *feng shui*, which is often considered to be superstitious and irrational, is not officially condoned or taken into account. It is possible however that on an informal and possibly even unconscious level, through personal and cultural influences, *feng shui* has some effect on various government activities. Nevertheless, it is clear that government control of planning and development would severely limit any geomantic influence that might have occurred in the wider landscape.

Feng Shui and the Public

This book is not really about the public's perception of *feng shui* or how much it is used, rather it is about what *feng shui* is in Singapore: what geomancers and their clients do and believe. No formal research was undertaken to find out exactly what the general public thinks about *feng shui* but, during the research period, I had many opportunities to talk about it with Singaporeans, from taxi drivers, hairdressers and shop assistants to professional people. These informal discussions helped me gain insight into the attitudes that help to shape *feng shui* in Singapore. As well as this, I did quick telephone surveys of architects, interior designers and landscape architects to find out how much *feng shui* affects their businesses. The results of this less formal research were fascinating.

Very few Singaporeans readily admit to believing in *feng shui*, but many seem very interested in it. Most were surprised and fascinated to find that a foreigner was interested in the subject and quickly asked what I thought. Everyone wanted to know if I believed in it. All Chinese Singaporeans had heard of *feng shui* though, in most cases, their understanding of it was superficial. Most referred to lucky numbers and perhaps the positioning of doors or furniture. Few knew anything about the importance of landscape features. Only a few people I met by chance said that they believed strongly in *feng shui* and only two had been to a geomancer. However, both of these had consulted a geomancer more than once and one had both his home and office examined and rearranged according to geomantic advice.

I talked with five architects, few of whom had any contact with geomancers. All together, only six clients had wanted geomantic involvement in their projects in the previous five years. This represents less than one percent of the architects' total business.

All the landscape designers had some contact with *feng shui* in their work. Mostly they said that only a few clients required geomancy to be taken into account. In about eight percent of their cases, on average, the client requested that advice be sought from a geomancer.

It is much more common for interior designers to have had *feng shui* influence their work. I asked each interior designer how many of their clients had geomancers help to advise on their projects. The smallest incidence was ten percent and the largest seventy percent. Overall, about one out of every three interior projects done by the designers interviewed included input from a geomancer. The vast majority of these cases were business premises, though some were in private homes.

This brief survey lends further weight to the conclusion that interior design is the main area in which *feng shui* is being taken into account in Singapore, and that *feng shui* is primarily used in an attempt to solve problems rather than pre-empt them.

Feng Shui and the Media

One part of the public arena in which *feng shui* is frequently acknowledged is the media. Media attention to *feng shui* is apparent but not widespread. In 1990, a half-hour television documentary and a special feature in The Straits Times focused on the apparent increase in popularity of *feng shui* in Singapore. In both cases, the discussion of geomantic principles emphasised the methods associated with the *feng shui* compass, directions and on the fortune telling aspects of *feng shui* rather than on aspects relating to auspicious landscapes and locational choice.

Another minor article in the Straits Times on 27 January 1990 quoted a number of university lecturers criticising the use of *feng shui*. It quotes a Dr Tang saying, "*feng shui* is part of the Chinese tradition and it is an art in itself. But people should not indulge in it . . . it is good to preserve some Chinese traditions but people have got to be more selective." *Feng shui* was also the subject of five cartoon strips in the "House of Lim" series by Cheah which appeared in the Straits Times between 5 and 9 March 1990. These presented an image of *feng shui* as old fashioned and silly, albeit in a very humorous way.

Arguments about whether *feng shui* is based on fact or superstition have been occurring among Chinese populations for hundreds of years. While many people are curious about *feng shui* and some take it very seriously, in public most will deride it as irrational and unconvincing. One very successful geomancer advertises that he will produce designs in which it is not obvious that *feng shui* has been used, for people who do not want to be seen to be practising it. Singaporeans seem torn between accepting *feng shui* as a traditional Chinese practice and rejecting it as unscientific.

Regardless of this dilemma and any degree of official discouragement, there is considerable public appeal in *feng shui*. Citibank ran two full page advertisements for home loans depicting ideal geomantic landscapes in the Straits Times on five occasions between 16 July and 14 August 1990. It seems likely, then, that Singaporeans are aware of the use of *feng shui* for identifying auspicious locations, however rare their opportunities may be for using it in this way.

While the geomantic tradition in Singapore seems to have been quite weak until recent years, it is clear that the discipline is widely known by Singaporeans, at least as a method of adapting given sites to given users. It also appears that something of a boom is occurring in the number of people who are actively involved in *feng shui* practice, that is, the geomancers and their clients. It is even possible that with increasing locational choices available to Singaporeans, through a degree of government deregulation and increased affluence, the methods of landscape analysis may become more popular. Whether the future of *feng shui* will tend towards its traditional form, emphasising a holistic universe, balance and harmony with nature, or instead towards the development of a hybrid, incorporating Western mechanistic and scientific values, has yet to be seen.

6
GEOMANCY AND ENVIRONMENTAL IDEAS

In recent years, a wave of concern for the natural environment has been building in many nations of the world. Most people are aware of growing problems associated with waste disposal, the accelerated greenhouse effect, depletion of the ozone layer and the loss of natural habitats and species diversity through such actions as the felling of the rainforests. Environmental scientists and others have come to fear that the world could be on its way to an environmental crisis which, if not stopped or tempered, could jeopardise the ability of the planet to sustain human life. Certainly, most would now accept that environmental degradation could at least compromise our ability to maintain our current quality of life, and undermine our attempts to improve the conditions of the millions who live in poverty, illness or hunger.

Human behaviour toward the environment (how we exploit or protect it) is based on our environmental ideas or attitudes. While individuals and cultures have varying attitudes toward the natural environment, it has become very important that all people re-evaluate the way in which we view the natural world and how we live within it.

Modern ideas of industrial, economic and technological progress are founded on two deeply held attitudes which help make way for an exploitative and destructive relationship with nature. First, humanity is considered to be somehow separate from and superior to nature with a right, even a duty, to change and dominate it. Second, we believe that science can unlock the secrets of nature and render them into totally understandable and predictable laws.

Through disciplines such as chemistry and physics, natural forces are dissected into formulae which are supposed to give us the power to predict how the environment will respond to any human interference. Modern Western society is based on the belief that we have not only the right but also the power to control nature. This so called technocentric view is that, through the use of new technology, humanity has absolute power over the environment and can manipulate it totally to whatever end is desired. Paradoxically, many of the same people who advocate the technocentric approach rely on an underlying faith that nature is so big and so powerful that humanity cannot really do it any damage.

While most people would consider these ideas to be extreme and unrealistic, recent exploitation and destruction of the natural environment has been allowed to proceed upon scientific assumptions which too narrowly define the area of impact of a development and then ignore or exclude uncertainties. The enormous complexity and interrelatedness of nature is avoided on a theoretical level because it is simply too difficult to deal with. Consequently, many models used for environmental impact assessment are frighteningly narrow and incomplete. While on the surface, analysis methods seem to offer predictability and control, the underlying fact is that much is left out because it is far too complex to fully comprehend, let alone incorporate. As a result, damaging interferences in the environment can often proceed on the pretence that we understand their effect, when in fact what we truly know and understand is only a small part of the overall situation. As evidence of serious environmental damage mounts up, it becomes clearer that such simplistic methods have to be discarded. The only sensible approach to uncertainty is caution.

In China, *feng shui* traditionally played some role in regulating the relationship between humanity and nature by encouraging an attitude of caution about human impact on the environment and allowing environmental modification only if it was not considered to disrupt natural balances and harmonies. Geomantic principles could be applied over both large and small areas. They were used in planning and building cities, in choosing sites for houses or burial grounds and orientating rooms or graves.

The purpose of geomancy was to identify places of high environmental quality. Using modern English terminology, aspect, water resources, fertility, vegetation, soil stability and lack of pollution were vitally important in this analysis, along with the directions, hexagrams, elements and other more esoteric factors. Certainly, once they were found, these places were used by people and this inevitably would result in some impact on the environment. But according to the principles of classical geomancy, changes to the natural state were to be undertaken with great care and kept to a minimum.

In *feng shui* theory, the environment is considered to be a highly complex living whole. All parts are intrinsically connected and the balances between them are delicate. Harmony between all elements of nature, including humanity, must be protected and consequently the fundamental attitudes to nature expressed in *feng shui* are respect and caution. These basic ideas have been found in *feng shui* from its beginnings and may provide us with insight, even solutions, to the problems we are now faced with.

Knowledge and Uncertainty in Environmental Approaches

One way in which contemporary technocentric societies can learn from *feng shui* to the benefit of the environment and future generations is in relation to our beliefs about knowledge and certainty. The way that we approach the environment is based on our world view: the sum of our beliefs about the world based on stories, formal education and other communications about the relationship between humanity and nature. This world view, which guides the way we treat the environment, is made up of a mixture of myth and theory. But what, really, is the difference between the two? And beyond that, do we recognise the difference between theory and reality?

In the modern Western tradition, scientific theory has been reified: theory is treated as truth. Western science is preoccupied with a search for the definition of physical reality. Not long ago (on the timeline of human civilisations) we believed that the sun and all other heavenly bodies rotated around the earth. By examining the history of "science" we find that its ideas (so called "laws") constantly change. Though it is often forgotten, one of the basic rules of science is that no theory can ever be proved to be true. Instead, the basis of the scientific method is that we learn about reality by disproving false theories. What is accepted theory today is merely a step (and possibly a misguided one) on the way towards greater understanding.

The way science is generally taught and used, however, encourages the belief that its current explanations of the natural world are the absolute truth. The Western tradition creates an ideology of science as reality and this, unfortunately, is a dominant part of our world view. Western scientific theory is now so prevalent that it is widely considered to describe physical reality with absolute precision. The traditional theories of other cultures, such as *feng shui*, are denigrated as myth or superstition.

It is vital to remember that, despite different methods of experimentation, deduction and proof, the conceptual approaches to the universe of both Chinese and Western cultures are, of course, entirely theoretical.

In *feng shui*, understanding of the universe is considered to be achieved through recognition of unity. The Western scientific method of proof by definition and dissection is anathema to this approach. Hence *feng shui*, through its philosophical nature, is vulnerable to the kinds of criticism levelled at it by Western commentators such as De Groot who wrote in 1897: "... natural philosophy in that part of the globe [China] is a huge mount of learning without a single trace of true knowledge in it."

Many previous Western studies have judged *feng shui* by supposedly scientific standards and thus created a conflict. Based on a false idea of what science itself is, these studies have declared *feng shui* at best pseudo-science and at worst superstition. That conflict appears to have been internalised in the ideas and practices of some geomancers in Singapore and by the Singaporean community which has not yet resolved whether to accept *feng shui* as traditional Chinese natural theory or to reject it as irrational and "unscientific".

A fundamental difference between the geomantic approach and that of Western science is that most geomancers acknowledge and understand that human interpretations of natural laws are theoretical rather than real. Most Singaporean geomancers readily accept that their interpretations of the cosmos, the forces of nature and consequently their analysis of the geomantic landscape, are indeed theoretical and that their theories may develop or change in the light of new evidence. There is also acceptance that different geomancers have different explanations for geomantic phenomena. It is very rare for geomancers to state unequivocally that they themselves are right while others are wrong. What is important is what seems to work and what results are achieved.

The ideology of reality encouraged in the Western tradition makes way for a strong belief in our ability to predict and control natural processes, whereas the traditional Chinese acceptance of the uncertain nature of human understanding of the environment encourages an attitude of respect and caution. Interestingly, in contemporary Singapore where Western scientific approaches are widely accepted, some geomancers and their clients express a desire for scientific verification of geomantic principles and one geomancer is developing more and more elaborate compasses and instruments for use in his practice. This is perhaps a result of the penetration of a mechanistic view of nature and the Western ideology of reality.

Another geomancer would not participate in the study because he claimed that he practised a scientific and correct form of *feng shui* and would not allow his views to be presented along with the differing ideas of other geomancers. Clearly, he has adopted the Western environmental ideology of scientific reality and incorporated it into his approach to *feng shui*.

This attempt to apply scientific method to geomantic practice encourages the misconceived notion that the use of scientific tools, such as elaborate compasses, makes geomantic practice less subjective. The theories of the forces of nature, on which all geomantic methodology is based, are of course entirely subjective. No introduced tool or method designed to "accurately" measure the influences of the five elements and the hexagrams can be considered to be objective.

This is not to say *feng shui* is invalid in any way, but where Singaporean geomancers are adopting Western mechanistic approaches to the environment, they are in danger of falling into the trap of trying to create formulae for the measurement of intangibles. By doing so they not only undermine the internal integrity of the system of *feng shui* but also further endanger the environment through introducing another tool which allows people to pretend that nature is entirely predictable and controllable. This synthesis of *feng shui* with supposedly scientific ideas could destroy *feng shui* as a theory of environmental protection. Rather than *feng shui* accommodating the modern Western approach, it would be preferable that the opposite occurred. It is essential that the caution and respect for the environment apparent in traditional *feng shui* theory are reintroduced into our world view and applied in all our activities.

Power and Control in the Human-Nature Relationship

Regardless of different cultures' concepts of the universe, their experience of the environment is the same at a basic level. All people seek to control their relationship with nature to some extent, whether it be by choosing a safe and comfortable abode, hunting or growing crops, or by diverting water, building power stations or genetically manipulating species. What varies is the degree of influence a culture perceives itself as having over nature and the level of impact on nature that is acceptable to it.

Superficially, traditional geomantic theory seems to imply that nature dominates humanity. The astrological makeup of a person is fundamental to their fate and their relationship with the environment. These birth characteristics are considered immutable and it would be easy to think that because of this a person's entire life path was predetermined.

Landscape is also considered to have a profound effect on the fate of its human inhabitants. The character of the landscape determines the availability of *sheng qi* and the auspiciousness of a site for any occupier. Different landscape configurations are considered to produce different kinds of fortune. As a result of this, however, classical *feng shui* is supposed to give people some power to determine their fate. In *feng shui*, if you understand nature and can align yourself with its forces, you will benefit. If you align yourself badly, or damage the environment, you, your family, your descendants and possibly your community will suffer.

Contemporary geomantic belief in Singapore strongly emphasises both the power of nature to affect human fate and the ability of humanity to control nature. All the geomancers interviewed believe that the influences of the astrological bodies totally determine certain aspects of an individual's character. This is not through any supernatural or spiritual power: the stars are considered part of the physical environment which is directly bound to the earth and the physical forces around us.

Astrological influences and the flow of *qi* are often put together in the catch-all phrase "magnetic fields" by many Singaporean geomancers. These magnetic fields are considered to be a very strong determiner of human fate. Human choice or free will is considered to operate within the general restrictions created by these fields.

One geomancer explained his attitude to free will with an allegorical tale:

> "You may not think that the planets' influence can influence you on earth. It is so far away how can it influence me? Forces that you cannot see are still forces. In the ocean there are a lot of currents, some currents from the north pole will bring you to the equator and so on. A lot of people will tell you that human beings have a free mind, given by God. I will say yes, to a certain degree.

"We look at a fish staying at the north pole, he is a very contented fish. He cannot see the water he is swimming in like we cannot see the air we are living in. He swims about and one day he swims from the small current into the big current. He doesn't know he went into the current because he can't see the water and he moves around within the current thinking he has a lot of free will.

'If I want to turn left I turn left, if I want to turn right I turn right. I can swim here or swim there, up to me.'

"But no, he is living in a force so big, which he cannot see, that he didn't even know he was in it. So eventually he will end up at the equator, thinking that he has a lot of free will."

The magnetic fields are considered to affect all aspects of a person's life, but in fact this doesn't mean that people have no control over their fate at all. The Singaporean approach to *feng shui* emphasises that, by adapting the places that people live and work in to the cosmological forces surrounding them, it is possible to maximise beneficial effects, or at least minimise negative influences.

While the geomancers are prepared to say that there are a lot of environmental influences that are beyond their and their clients' control, they also claim that it is very rare for a situation to be irredeemable. Singaporean *feng shui* seems to emphasise the ability of humans to control or change nature to our advantage more than the classical system, which is much more concerned with discovering whether a place is good or bad. Traditionally, if the *feng shui* of a place was considered to be bad, the client simply would not stay there rather than try to change it.

There were also moral questions about using *feng shui* in traditional times. There is evidence of a controversy about whether or not people should intervene in their own destiny by manipulating natural forces. Some writers objected on the basis that human fate should be left for heaven to determine, claiming that heaven would reward the virtuous by leading them to auspicious sites without active attempts on their part.[1] The argument focused on whether or not people should, not could, intervene in their own fate. That it was possible was accepted.

It would be highly unlikely in traditional circumstances that a geomancer

---

[1] March, 1968.

would assert that the influence of humanity could actually dominate nature. Nature was considered to set boundaries within which people could determine the course of their lives. It was not believed that auspicious sites could be completely created, though they could easily be destroyed, by humanity. *Feng shui* was a mechanism through which people determined how to develop the environment in ways that suited them, while maintaining the perceived balance and harmony in nature.

While human fate is not considered to be entirely determined by nature, the ability of humans to affect their own fate is dependant on adaptation to and manipulation of natural forces, not on any ability to change them.

The belief in the ability to adjust sites to the cosmological forces is very strong in Singapore. Singaporean geomancers consider that it is the role of the geomancer to make the best use of any given site. Recommendations regarding the location, or relocation, of accommodation are made very infrequently. This does not imply that Singaporean geomancers believe that humans can dominate nature, rather they have developed their methods for adapting sites and increased their belief in the ability of people to organise any site so that beneficial forces prevail.

Singaporean geomancers, however, generally consider the cosmological forces to be much more important than the influence of landscape. They believe that the role of landscape in determining the fate of its inhabitants can be substantially or totally mitigated by orientation and the use of remedies. In modern environmental terms, this perhaps liberates *feng shui* too much from the constraints which might previously have protected the environment. Geomancers in Singapore are primarily concerned with organising the physical environment which the client has power to control, usually within the very limited boundaries of their own apartment, house or office, and to filter the influences of nature so that positive forces prevail and negative forces are deflected. The extreme emphasis of this part of geomantic practice is quite different from the traditional, more ecological, approach.

A consequence of this, perhaps, is some geomancers' belief that auspicious environments can actually be created. This is a point of disagreement among Singaporean geomancers and it represents a profound divergence from traditional beliefs. One geomancer stated that reclaimed land could not be auspicious because it was artificial and had no *qi*. Another considered that in general reclaimed land was not as good as natural land but it was not all bad because it is by the sea which is beneficial. Reclaiming land could also be interpreted as a sign of prosperity "like putting on weight – but you must be careful not to strain the heart". This geomancer added, however, that the Chinese saying "you should not add legs to a snake" (do not try to improve what is already perfect) was generally applicable.

In contrast, most other geomancers believed that reclaimed land could be as auspicious as natural land primarily if the directions and elements were auspicious. One considered that the image of the land was important and cited the case of the reclaimed land at Marina South which he considers to be very auspicious because it is shaped like a bull's head and horns.

All of these geomancers stated that auspicious sites could be created by humans. Creation of auspicious sites is still, however, dependant on the careful analysis and manipulation of natural forces. This indicates a strong belief in the ability of humanity to manipulate the influences of nature, but not in the absolute dominance of humanity over nature.

As seen above, the relationship between nature and humanity as represented in *feng shui* is very complex. It does not offer a simplistic analysis such as "humanity controls nature" or "nature controls humanity". The basic idea is that humanity and nature interact. We affect each other, in fact, we are each other.

Traditional Chinese philosophies always emphasised holism and, unlike Western environmental philosophy, in *feng shui*, humanity is considered a functional part of nature. Human interests and influences are subsumed in the greater whole.

The Holistic Approach to the Environment

Discussing *feng shui* purely in terms of European ideas about the relationship between nature and humanity is ultimately unsuccessful because of the strong dualism in the Western approach. In *feng shui*, humanity and nature are part of a whole. The relationship is not strictly differentiated as each is seen to exist within a greater unity, whereas in the Western ideologies of environmental determinism (the idea that the environment totally determines human conditions and characteristics) and technocentrism (in which human technology is considered to be able to overcome any environmental obstacle), humanity and nature are seen as quite separate entities.

In *feng shui*, the essential unity of all things is fundamental. Every thing, natural or constructed, animate or inanimate, is a product of the forces of the universe and itself exerts influence in the universe. All of these forces are considered to be not only mutually influential but connected at the most basic level.

One geomancer states that after years of meditation he began to see the force that he had read so much about. It was clear to him that the meridians of energy which flow through the human body, and are the basis of the theories of acupuncture, were the same as the meridians of energy in the land. This geomancer drew the analogy between auspicious sites in the landscape where *qi* accumulates and the acupuncture points of the body. He also considered the whole universe to be a product of this energy which he described as "life force". Another very influential geomancer practiced *qi gong* for many years and also emphasised the importance of this fundamental "energy" which animates the universe and determines the health and fate of all people.

Chinese philosophy, mythology and many folk stories show that the delineation between humanity and nature is unclear in traditional Chinese thought. In the Chinese tradition and in *feng shui* there is no distinction between animate and inanimate, god and creation, humanity and nature. Humanity is a part of nature and has a mutual relationship of influence with all other agents in nature. In traditional Chinese painting, humans and human-made objects were always set in dominating natural landscapes. In religious practice, meditation on nature brought people closer to their spiritual essence.

By contrast, in the Western, and particularly the Christian, tradition there has been acceptance, in fact advocacy, of duality. Between God and Creation, humanity and nature, animate and inanimate things, the emphasis has been on difference and separateness. "Man" is given domain over nature. His task is to watch over and perfect nature, helping God to complete His creation. There is no question that animals and all other forms of life are considered lower than "Man".

Singaporean geomancers and their clients accept that humans and human structures are both subject to the forces of the environment and are forces in the environment. In *Case Eight*, Chapter Three we saw that the revolving restaurant below the solicitor's window forms his mandarin's seal, which is a beneficial force. The environment which influences him is made up of both natural and human-made features.

All the geomancers stated that in an urban environment human structures can perform the functions traditionally associated with features of the natural environment: buildings can play the role of mountains by protecting auspicious sites, roads can be like rivers or act as sources of *qi*. Major transportation routes are considered to be dragons. Human structures are an integral part of the landscape in *feng shui* and the influence between nature and humanity is seen to be reciprocal. Hence for the wellbeing of society and its members, interferences in the natural environment should be undertaken with great care and forethought.

Traditionally, it was considered that while nature imposes certain absolute limits, the relationship of nature and humanity is interactive. There was a particularly strong awareness of the possibility of human activity having negative influences on the environment which could either disturb the balance of nature or destroy the qualities of a site and consequently harm its inhabitants. It was also believed that such damage could often be rectified through careful remedial action.

Singaporean geomancers also believe that human impact on the environment can have serious negative effects on the geomantic qualities of the landscape and its occupants, and that such damage can be reversed. A story commonly cited by geomancers relates to the Singapore River. In the mid 1980s, land was reclaimed outside the natural mouth of the Singapore River and this was considered to result in less *sheng qi* being delivered to the financial district, causing a downturn in the economy. The Merlion fountain was subsequently constructed at the original mouth of the river (**Photo 13**). Geomancers state that this rectified the situation by keeping the water moving in the area and so the *qi* would not stagnate. The Merlion is also said to guard the wealth of the city.

Clearly, in contemporary Singapore, *feng shui* theory still incorporates the idea that humanity and nature have a relationship of mutual influence, but perhaps the fundamental bonds have been loosened. *Feng shui* practice is essentially driven by self interest and geomancers have to find solutions which allow people to do what they want to do or they won't be paid. In ancient China, where population density was lower and human development of the landscape less dramatic, it would have been easier to accommodate the desires of individuals without severely or immediately damaging the environment. As much as *feng shui* issued guidelines and warnings for people in their relationship with the environment, development still went ahead and cumulatively significant environmental damage was done. As early as the Chou dynasty, concerns were being raised about deforestation and its potential effects, particularly increased flooding.

Similarly in modern times, by narrowing one's view and applying *feng shui* in a way which is intended to maximise the benefit to the individual who wants his or her house built or commercial development to go ahead, the holistic approach has often enough been disregarded. For *feng shui* to re-emerge as a wise and useful means of environmental protection, emphasis must again be placed on its holism. The actions of all individuals affect the whole environment. We must accept that short term individual gain which is based on environmental degradation leads to long term general loss.

In the last two centuries of contact with Western technology and culture, Chinese culture has faced a barrage of challenges. It could be argued that a significant change in world view is occurring. "Modernisation" programmes throughout the Oriental world are based on the adoption of Western technologies. If the mechanistic interpretation of the physical world which underlies these technologies is fully adopted, nothing less than a paradigm shift will have occurred in the Oriental world and an important source of wisdom about the environment will be lost.

Traditionally, *feng shui* revered nature, counselled caution in interfering with the environment and always aimed to maintain natural balances and harmony. Some Singaporean geomancers also advocate this philosophy. This does not mean they are necessarily against development. Most geomancers state that although it is much more difficult to maintain beneficial balances in densely built and populated areas, it is still possible. Any individual building or modification of the environment is not intrinsically negative. It is the relationship of each development to the existing environment which determines whether the effect will be beneficial or destructive.

Whereas in nature wastes are broken down and recycled through ecosystems so that natural balances are maintained, industrial and other human waste products are often dumped and may not degrade for hundreds or even thousands of years. Pollution of all kinds is considered to result in an imbalance of the five elements. Where the elements are out of balance, a place is sick and it can only result in illness for the people who live there.

Nevertheless, it appears that in general Singaporean geomancers have a stronger belief in the ability of humans to regulate their relationship with nature than their traditional Chinese predecessors. While the fundamental ideas remain, what has changed is the perception of the balance of power.

There are three factors which, individually or in combination, may account for this divergence from traditional approaches. The first is the limitation on locational choice. Because individuals have limited control over locations, more non-ideal sites must be rendered habitable through the use of compass techniques. This results in a greater sense of human ability to manipulate nature than is apparent traditionally. In general, geomantic practice has adapted to the limitations imposed in Singapore. One retired geomancer, however, gave up his practice partly because of his belief that there was so little that could be done in the urban environment and that geomantic practice was severely undermined and misused.

The second possible factor is the adoption of Western technocentric and scientific ideologies which also assume a greater degree of power over nature. Thirdly, it follows that as a community becomes urbanised and industrialised, the sense of closeness between people and nature is undermined. It may be that Singaporean geomancers are developing not only a belief in their ability to control the influences of nature but also a growing sense of humanity's separateness from nature.

Certainly the balance of power between humanity and nature does appear to have changed in recent history. Technology has empowered people to radically alter the way that many of us live and has changed the face of the earth, but recent discoveries show that this process cannot continue forever. The beliefs that humanity has unlimited power to control nature and that technology can overcome all environmental problems now appears hopelessly naive.

The discovery of the hole in the ozone layer is a good example to illustrate this. At first there was amazement that we could unintentionally cause such damage to this essential shield for the planet. Yes, even indirectly human activities can have a profound and potentially disastrous effect on the natural balances and systems of our environment. Then, after accepting that this process is occurring, scientists have repeatedly claimed that they can identify the specific causes and predict rates of deterioration. Every year these predictions are proven wrong (the damage has been consistently underestimated and the hole is found to be bigger than expected), new theories are put forward and new predictions are made.

What we must accept and adapt to is the knowledge that natural systems are enormously complex and interrelated, and as such are largely unpredictable. For instance, meteorologists now admit that long term weather prediction is a very unreliable sport. Modern science and philosophy are beginning to develop or rediscover approaches which accept this unpredictability, such as Chaos Theory and the Gaia Principle (based on the ancient Greek idea that the earth as a whole is a living, organic unit). These ideas, however, are still very much on the fringe of accepted science, far from being adopted into general practice.

Their underlying messages are easy to grasp and should not be difficult to adopt. Respect the environment in which we live. Interfere in it with great caution. Accept that we do not fully understand it and certainly cannot control it and so, minimise human impact on it. Learn, again, to live in harmony with the environment so as not to disrupt its very delicate natural balances.

In recent years, Singapore's government has embarked on an environmental awareness campaign and public concern about the environment is deepening. Through recognition that Chinese culture has its own tradition of environmental awareness and ecological protection, *feng shui* could become a valuable asset in this movement.

APPENDIX ONE
CONCLUSIONS

In this appendix, I present a brief summary of the academic findings of the research for those who may be interested. As I said in the introduction, this can only be considered to be a preliminary study of geomancy in Singapore. I am sure that as a result more questions have been asked than answered. At least, now, we have some idea of the nature of geomancy in Singapore and why it has been left out of the academic literature. I hope that any future researchers might find some value in these conclusions. They present Singaporean *feng shui* as very dynamic, possibly undergoing fundamental changes at the time of this study. I look forward with great interest to the results of any comprehensive survey of geomantic beliefs and practices in Singapore.

The Theoretical Foundations of Singaporean Geomancers' Practices

Most of the fundamental principles of traditional geomancy are incorporated into the theoretical approaches of Singaporean geomancers. All but one of the geomancers interviewed discussed the components of auspicious landscapes based on the traditional principles of auspiciousness, including the accumulation of qi, protective mountain ranges and access to water, and all geomancers were familiar with the range of cosmological systems which are the basis of the practices of analysing the relationships between people and sites and between different objects in the environment. All geomancers used the geomancy compass for the assessment of sites and the Chinese almanac to determine auspicious dates.

An important characteristic of Singaporean *feng shui* is the non-traditional relationship between the theories of landscape and site analysis. Whereas in a traditional situation they would be used hand in hand, perhaps with emphasis on the landscape aspects of the analysis, in Singapore cosmological influences on specific sites dominate geomantic practice, at times to the exclusion of landscape analysis. This is a significant divergence from tradition.

Modern adaptations of the traditional theory are also very common in

Singapore. All geomancers stated that features of the urban environment could be considered to take on the roles attributed to natural environmental elements in the traditional system. For example, buildings can be treated as mountains and roads can be considered rivers. This phenomenon has also been reported by authors concentrating on geomantic practice in Hong Kong, such as Freedman and Skinner.

There is some disagreement between geomancers in Singapore with regard to certain aspects of geomantic theory. For example, geomancers disagree about the value of auspicious burial in determining the fortunes of descendants and about whether geomantic principles apply when the dead are cremated.

Geomancers also disagree about the extent to which landscape modification affects the geomantic values of sites. Some consider that the urbanisation process has been detrimental to the geomantic character of Singapore, while others state that this has not been a general effect, but is dependant on the configurations of the elements which affect different people in different ways. Disagreement also appeared in the evaluation of the geomantic qualities of reclaimed land.

Disagreement between geomancers has been documented in previous studies, and this in itself is not a unique feature of geomancy in Singapore. The nature of some of the theoretical divergences, however, indicates that Singaporean geomantic thought may be adapting to modern and even local circumstances.

The Nature of Singaporean Geomantic Consultancies

Most of the consultancies run by the geomancers interviewed were run as commercial enterprises and some use commercial advertising and media publicity to create a market and draw clients.

Few geomancers served traditional or long term apprenticeships to acquire their geomantic knowledge and skills. This could further explain apparent theoretical divergences from tradition.

The professional practice of geomancy includes a very small number of cases where geomancers are engaged to assess a site before it is bought or rented, a larger minority of cases where geomantic principles are included in the design stage of building construction or interior decoration and a majority of cases in which premises already occupied are assessed by geomancers.

The majority of clients seek geomantic advice because of a perceived problem. Mostly these are business related, though family and health problems are also common reasons for consultation. Clients do not appear to consult with geomancers because they directly perceive that the geomantic characteristics of the premises are deficient.

The most common actions recommended by geomancers and undertaken by clients involve the rearrangement of furniture and household fixtures, with the intention of harmonising the prevailing elements, and using remedies such as lion statuettes to deflect negative influences. Structural changes are made in a very small number of cases.

Analysis of Landscape and Location

Geomancers' analyses and discussions of the landscape are relatively superficial, though most analysed the landscape of Singapore in traditional terms such as the positions of dragons and water bodies. Personified images of the landscape are also in evidence, though not as abundantly as would be expected in an Oriental city with a strong geomantic tradition.

As geomancy is infrequently used to locate buildings in Singapore, its most obviously geographic aspect, i.e. a locational effect, appears to be very limited.

Environmental Attitudes

The environmental attitudes expressed through the geomantic principles and practices of Singaporean geomancers are fundamentally those traditionally associated with geomancy. Most Singaporean geomancers see the human relationship to nature as not merely interactive, but integral. There is evidence, however, that Singaporean geomancers perceive humans to exert a greater degree of influence in their relationship with the environment than is reported in other studies of geomantic practice. There is also a greater emphasis on the cosmological influences affecting a site than the influences of the surrounding landscape.

These changes in emphasis in the environmental attitudes displayed may be symptomatic of a more profound shift. Some Singaporean geomancers seem to be accommodating Western scientific perceptions of the universe, particularly with regard to the need or ability to scientifically define and empirically "prove" geomantic phenomena.

Theoretical Divergence from Norms Identified in Previous Studies

As can be seen above, there is some evidence that Singaporean geomantic theory diverges from traditional norms and those identified in recent studies in other places such as Hong Kong and Korea. A spectrum of opinion is apparent among geomancers in Singapore which appears to encompass greater variation than that reported in other studies. This may be due to a tendency in other studies only to report the more generally held opinions of geomancers, or it could be a result of a relatively weak geomantic tradition in Singapore.

The emphasis on the cosmological concerns of the Compass School is evidence of divergence from traditional geomantic practice. Relatively recent work concentrating on geomantic practice in Hong Kong, however, also reflects an emphasis on the compass aspects of geomancy. It seems logical that this emphasis will occur in built up environments where locational choice is limited and landscape features are relatively obscured. In Singapore, the emphasis of compass methods is extreme and the de-emphasis of the influence of landscape is very apparent. This may be a result of the further limitations of locational choice imposed by the Singaporean government.

The belief held by many geomancers that auspicious sites can be created represents a strong divergence from the findings of previous studies. With the extreme emphasis of the compass methods, a greater perception of the ability to control the influences of the environment may ensue. This belief in the greater ability of humans to control nature may also be a result of contact with and adoption of Western technocentric approaches as discussed above.

The Geomantic Tradition in Singapore

It is apparent that the practice of geomancy is currently in a period of increase, possibly resurgence, in Singapore. To some extent Singaporean geomancy is a distinct form. It is difficult in the apex of change to see the final direction or form it may take. If in the future, due to greater affluence and education of the population and further deregulation of locational controls by government, the choice of locations becomes an important part of geomantic practice in Singapore it is possible that a return to more traditional theories, and the environmental attitudes which underpin them, may occur. If, however, further integration of Western scientific approaches occurs through, for example, the empirical research of geomantic phenomena advocated by some geomancers and clients, a more idiosyncratic and untraditional variety of geomancy may result.

APPENDIX TWO
LIST OF GEOMANCERS INTERVIEWED

Geomancer's Name	Company and Address
Cheong, Danny	Danny Cheong Company Towner Road PO Box 1485
Ee, H P (Albert)	15 Still Road South
Gwee, Peter	Fulu Geomancy Centre #02–06 Katong Shopping Centre
Koh, George	Paramount Astrology #01–36 Paramount Shopping Centre
Koh, Kenny	Tend Tao Tang Geomancy Centre #05–37 Bukit Timah Centre
Lim Koon Hian	San Yen Geomancy Centre #03–47 Parkway Parade
Lip Mong Har (Evelyn)	National University of Singapore, Kent Ridge Crescent
Tan Koon Yong	Way Geomancy Centre #02–10 Fulu Shou Complex
Wong, Jimmy	No longer practising
Wong Loy Hin	Zhong Hua Geomancy 490A Changi Rd

GLOSSARY

Ba Gua	The Eight Trigrams
Dao	Literally "the Way", the undifferentiated state of the universe. (Also *Tao*).
Daoism	The philophy of Daoism (Taoism) as expounded by Lao Ze (c. 600BC) and others.
Dao De Jing	*The Classic of the Way and its Virtue* attributed to Lao Ze.
Feng	Wind
Feng Shui	Literally "Wind and Water"; Geomancy.
I Jing	*The Book of Changes*, containing the philosphy of the Eight Trigrams and 64 Hexagrams. (Also *I Ching*).
Li	Principle; the principle or blueprint of all components of the universe.
Long	Dragon.
Luo Pan	The Geomancy Compass.
Qi	Energy; the mass/energy/life force that animates the universe.
Qi Kou	Literally "energy mouth"; the point at which *qi* enters a given area.
Qi Gong	A traditional Chinese martial art designed to enhance the flow of *qi* within the body.
Sha Qi	Literally "death energy"; *qi* in a destructive form.
Sheng Qi	Literally "life energy"; *qi* in a beneficial form.
Shui	Water.
Tai Ji	The Great Ultimate, encompassing *Dao* and *Yin-Yang*.

Wu Xing	The Five Elements or Five Moving Agents.
Yang	One of the two opposite forces in nature which make up *Dao*. *Yang* implies the forceful, bright, warm aspects of all things.
Yin	One of the two opposite forces in nature which make up *Dao*. *Yin* implies the yeilding, dark, cool aspects of all things.
Zuo Shan Xiang Hai	Literally "Sitting on [the side of] a mountain facing the sea"; an expression of an ideal geomantic situation.

BIBLIOGRAPHY

Chan Wing-Tsit, 1969: *A Source Book in Chinese Philosophy*, Princeton University Press, Princeton.

Cheong, Danny Rui-min, 1989: "Wind-Borne Luck, Water-Bourne Wealth: The Art of Fengshui or Chinese Geomancy", *Interior Digest*, Vol 7 No 2, Metropolitan Publishing, Singapore.

De Groot, J. J. M., 1897: *The Religious System of China*, Vol 3, Leiden: Librairie.

Eitel, Ernest J., 1984: *Feng Shui*, Graham Brash (Pte) Ltd, Singapore, (first published 1873, Lane Crawford and Co., Hong Kong).

Feuchtwang, Stephan D. R., 1974: *An Anthropological Analysis of Chinese Geomancy*, Vithagna, Taipei.

Forke, Alfred, 1925: *The World Conception of the Chinese: Their Astronomical, Cosmological and Physico-philosophical Speculations*, Arthur Probsthain, London.

Freedman, Maurice, 1968: "Geomancy", *Proceedings of the Royal Anthropological Institute of Great Britain and Ireland*, pp 5–15.

Freedman, Maurice, 1979: *The Study of Chinese Society: Essays by Maurice Freedman*, Stanford University Press, California.

Fung Yu-lan, 1960: *A Short History of Chinese Philosophy*, Macmillan Company, New York.

Ho Wing Leong David, 1989: "Chinese Geomancy: A Geographic Perspective in Singapore", Academic Exercise, Department of Geography, National University of Singapore, unpublished.

Lip Mong Har Evelyn, 1979: *Chinese Geomancy, A Layman's Guide to Feng Shui*, Times Books International, Singapore.

Lip Mong Har Evelyn, 1985: *Feng Shui for the Home*, Times Books International, Singapore.

Lip Mong Har Evelyn, 1989: *Feng Shui For Business*, Times Books International, Singapore.

March, Andrew L., 1968: "An Appreciation of Chinese Geomancy", *Journal of Asian Studies*, Vol. 27, pp 253–267.

March, Andrew L., 1974: *The Idea of China: Myth and Theory in Geographic Thought*, Praeger, New York.

Needham Joseph, 1956–1962: *Science and Civilisation in China*, Cambridge University Press, England, Vol 2, 1956 and Vol 4, 1962.

Popper, Karl, 1959: *The Logic of Scientific Discovery*, Hutchinson, London.

Rossbach, Sarah, 1983: *Feng Shui: The Chinese Art of Perfect Placement*, E.P. Dutton Inc. New York.

Skinner, Stephen, 1983: *The Living Earth Manual of Feng Shui, Chinese Geomancy*, Graham Brash (Pte) Ltd, Singapore.

Turnbull, Mary, 1977: *A History of Singapore 1819–1975*, Oxford University Press, Kuala Lumpur.

Urban Redevelopment Authority, 1990: *Skyline*, Vol. 6/90, Urban Redevelopment Authority, Singapore.

Walters, Derek, 1988: *Feng Shui: Perfect Placing for Your Happiness and Prosperity*, Asiapac, Singapore.

Wilhelm, Richard, 1952: *I Ching or Book of Changes*, Routledge Kegan and Paul, London.

Yoon, Hong-Key, 1976: "Geomantic Relationships between Culture and Nature in Korea", *Asian Folklore and Social Life Monographs*, No. 88, The Orient Cultural Service, Taipei.

Yoon, Hong-key, 1980: "The Image of Nature in Geomancy", *GeoJournal*, 4.4/1980.

Yoon, Hong-key, 1982: "Environmental Determinism and Geomancy: Two cultures, Two Concepts", *GeoJournal*, 6.1/1982.

Yoon, Hong-Key, 1985: "An Early Chinese Idea of a Dynamic Environmental Cycle", *GeoJournal*, 10.2/1985.

Yoon, Hong-key, 1986: "The Nature and Origin of Chinese Geomancy", *Eratosthene-Sphragide*, 1, pp. 88–102.

Yoon, Hong-key, 1990: "Loess Cave-Dwellings in Shaanxi Province, China", *GeoJournal*, 21.1/2.

INDEX

Acupuncture   95
Adaptation   93
Aesthetics   2, 14, 49, 50
Ancestor worship   4, 17
Ancestral altar   13, 42, 43
Angle   1, 40, 41–43, 48
Animal   1, 9, 11, 16, 17, 32, 41, 96
  azure dragon   62–64, 69, 70, 74, Fig. 8 (64)
  bird   1, 6, 16
  black tortoise   14
  crab   65, 66, Fig. 9 (66)
  dragon   1, 14, 16, 17, 25, 31, 50, 62–64, 69–75, 82, 96, 102, Fig. 11 (71)
  eagle   65, 67, 68, Fig. 10 (67)
  fish   46, 48, 63, 69, 75, 92
  lion   1, 13, 31, 47, 49
  red bird   16
  tiger   1, 13, 14, 16, 50, 62, 63, 64, 69, 70, 73–75, Fig. 8 (64)
  white tiger   14, 16, 62, 63, 64, 69, 70, 74
Apprentice   19, 20, 21, 33
Aquarium   52
Architecture   29, 30, 78
Aspect   3, 4, 9, 29, 30, 35, 37–49, 63, 69, 78, 80, 82, 84, 87, 91, 92, 100–103
Astrology   2, 8, 33, 78
  horoscope   41
  zodiac   11
Azure (see Colour)
Azure Dragon (see Animal)

Ba Gua (see Trigram)
Balance   2, 5, 16, 26, 29, 31–33, 85, 87, 93, 96, 97, 98, 99
Bank   1, 27, 34, 40–43, 51
Bed   12, 27, 28
Black (see Colour)
Bird (see Animal)
Black tortoise (see Animal)

Book of Changes (or *I Jing/I Ching*) 8, 106
Buddhism (see Religion)
Burial 17, 35, 36, 87
 cemetery 23, 35, 76, 77
 grave 4, 16, 18, 35, 87
Businesses 19, 22, 33, 34, 36, 83

Canals 47, 69
Cave (*xue*) 4, 14, 16, 73
 cave dwelling 4
Cemetery (see Burial)
China 1, 3, 4, 9, 17, 18, 20, 22, 23, 30, 35, 77, 82, 87, 89, 97
Chinese religion (see Religion)
Christianity (see Religion)
Colonist 63, 78
Colour 9, 11, 16, 30, 33, 39, 43–45, 51, 75, 81, 82
 azure 14, 16, 62, 63, 69, 70, 74
 black 5, 11, 14, 24, 25, 48, 82
 blue 6, 44, 52, 82
 green 11, 38, 39, 51, 75, 81
 red 9, 11, 16, 21, 35, 79, 80, 81
 white 5, 11, 14, 16, 50, 62, 82
 yellow 9, 11, 16, 43, 82
Compass (or *luo pan*) 9, 12–14, 37, 84, 90, 98, 100, 103
 Compass School 12–14, 22, 103
Conflict 9, 11–13, 63, 65, 82, 89
Conifer (see Tree)
Cooker 13, 43
 stove 42, 43
Cosmology 1, 2, 4, 5, 6
Crab (see Animal)
Cycle 6–9, 13

Dao/Daoism (see Religion)
Dates 8, 9, 43
Desk 1, 13, 41–44, 50
Dimensions 11, 42, 43, 46, 47, 51
Direction 9, 11–13, 37, 38, 43–45, 51, 70, 72, 74, 82, 84, 87, 94, Fig. 4 (11)
 centre 9, 11, 17, 23, 38, 51, 52, 63, 65, 68, 70, 72–74, 82

Direction (cont'd)
  east   9, 14, 26, 63, 65, 69, 70, 73, 82
  north 4, 9, 14, 16, 17, 62, 69, 70, 76, 82, 91, 92
  south 4, 9, 14, 16, 22, 44, 62, 63, 65, 69, 70, 72, 74, 75, 82, 94
  west   2, 6, 9, 14, 17, 18, 26, 44, 65, 69, 70
Divination   2, 8
Door   1, 11–13, 38–40, 41, 43–49, 77, 80, 83
Dragon (see Animal)
Drain   37, 47, 69

Eagle (see Animal)
Earth (see Element)
Ecology   2, 18
Economy   30, 31, 42, 96
Eight Trigrams (see Trigram)
Element   2, 3, 6–9, 11–13, 73, 74, 78, 87, 88, 90, 94, 98, 101, 102, Fig. 2 (7)
  earth   2, 6, 8, 9, 11, 17, 18, 32, 37, 43, 80, 88, 91, 98, 99
  fire   6, 8, 9, 17, 32, 37, 42, 43, 52
  metal   6, 8, 37, 46
  water   2, 4, 6, 16, 17, 32, 37, 42, 43, 46, 47, 50, 52, 63, 69, 87, 91, 92, 96
  wind   17, 62, 80
  wood   17, 32
Emotions   32, 48
Energy (see Qi)
Environment   1–3, 9, 11, 12, 13, 14, 18, 76, 77, 86, 87, 88, 89, 90, 91, 92, 93, 94, 95, 96, 97, 98, 99, 100, 101, 102, 103
Escalator   47, 50

Fate   2, 8, 11, 12, 91, 92, 93, 95
Fire (see Element)
Fish (see Animal)
Five Elements (see Element)
Food   18, 23, 38, 51, 63, 65, 68
Form School   12, 14, 61
Fortune   2, 8, 13, 14, 16, 18, 84, 91, 101
Fortune telling   2, 8, 84
Furniture   3, 11, 13, 34, 35, 41–43, 46, 50, 78, 83
  (see also Bed, Desk, Cooker)

Gaia   18, 99
Gate   22, 45, 46–49, 93
Geography   2, 65
Ghosts   49, 76
God (see Religion)
Goddess of Mercy (see Religion)
Government   29, 36, 63, 68, 72, 75, 77, 79, 82, 85, 99, 103, 104
Grave (see Burial)
Green (see Colour)

Happiness   3, 13, 51
Harmony   9, 30, 32, 85, 88, 93, 97, 99
Health   2, 13, 18, 28, 33, 69, 95, 102
Hexagram   9, 11, 12, 37, 44, 45, 87, 90
History   3, 74, 76, 78, 88, 98
Holistic   5, 16, 85, 94, 97
Hong Chun (Reverend)   19, 21, 40, 82
Hong Kong   3, 18, 24, 26, 27, 31, 34, 62, 101, 103
Horseshoe   14, 63, 74
Hotel   34, 40, 47, 73, 75, 80
Housing and Development Board (HDB)   74, 76, 77, 80

Ideal landscape   4, 14, 15, 17, 62, 63, 73, 74, Fig. 5 (15)
Ideal site   4, 14, 16, 17, 63, 73, 76
I Jing (*I Ching*) (see Book of Changes)
Illness   25, 28, 44, 86, 98
Indonesia   21, 62, 63

Job   19, 23–25, 27–29, 33, 42, 43

Kinship   79
Korea   3, 18, 20, 21, 35, 65, 77, 103

Lao Ze   2, 5, 8, 16
Law   3, 6, 11, 13, 86, 88, 89
Li   6
Lion (see Animal)
Location   1, 17, 61–63, 65, 76,–81, 84, 85, 93, 98
Loess Plateau   4, 9, 16
Long (see Animal, dragon)

Lowland 50
Luck 18, 23, 24, 28, 47, 48, 52
Luo pan (see Compass)

Magic 14, 50–52, 74
Magnetic fields 91, 92
Main mountain 14, 50, 62, 69, 70, 74
Malaysia 21, 62, 63, 69, 70, 72
Mass Rapid Transit (MRT) 21, 31, 75, 81, 82
Master plan 79, 80
Medicine 2, 27
Meditation 20, 31, 95
Metal (see Element)
Meridians 95
Merlion 21, 96
Mind 6, 23, 31–33, 76, 92
Mirror 1, 9, 13, 49
Mountain 2, 9, 14, 16, 17, 32, 50, 51, 62, 69, 70, 72, 73, 96, 100
Mythology 88, 95

Names 8
National University 78, 81
Natural environment 2, 3, 9, 86, 87, 96
New towns 80
Number 4, 6, 19, 22, 28, 30, 34, 36, 37, 38, 40–42, 45, 47, 49, 51, 52, 70, 72, 75, 80, 81, 83, 84, 85, 101, 102
  16 41, 51
  numerology 8, 33

Orchard Road 25, 52, 70, 73
Orientation 3, 9, 12, 13, 39, 46, 78, 93
Origin 3, 4, 22, 78

Painting 1, 13, 14, 51, 95
Philosophy 3, 18, 28, 89, 94, 95, 99
Planning 39, 79, 80, 82, 87
Pollution 32, 87, 98
Power lines 47.
Prosperity 3, 18, 30, 46, 63, 72, 79, 94
Psychology 2, 14

Qi   6, 12, 17, 18, 25, 46, 62, 63, 70, 72, 73, 75, 91, 94, 95, 96, 100, 106, Fig. 6 (39)
  deflect   3, 9, 13, 41, 46, 49, 50
  sha   2, 5, 8, 9, 13, 14, 23, 26, 30, 47, 48, 49, 62
  sheng   6, 12, 13, 14, 16, 17, 18, 62, 65, 69, 72, 91, 96
  vital energy   6, 16, 17
Qi gong   31, 95

Reclamation   41, 73
Red (see Colour)
Red bird (see Animal)
Religion   20, 21–25, 30
  Buddhist   20, 24
  Chinese religion   20, 21
  Christian   20, 95
  Dao   2, 5, 6, 16, 20
  Daoism   2, 5, 20
  god   5, 20, 27, 31, 32, 92, 95, 96
  Goddess of Mercy
Remedy   13, 24, 42, 43, 49
River   12, 21, 69, 70, 72, 74, 75, 96, 101
Road   1, 5, 13, 25, 47, 49, 52, 70, 72, 73, 74, 96
Ruler (Geomantic)   11, 46

Science   18, 82, 86, 88, 89, 99
Sea   14, 25, 31, 62, 63, 69, 70, 73, 74, 94
Sentosa   65
Sha qi (see Qi)
Sheng qi (see Qi)
Singapore River   21, 70, 72, 74, 75, 96
Staff   28, 33, 42, 44, 45, 51
Statue   1, 13, 21, 41, 47, 49, 102
Stove (see Cooker)
Straight lines   38, 47, 69
Structural change   43, 46, 81, 102
Superstition   84, 88, 89
Symbol   2, 5, 13, 14, 16, 38, 41, 46, 51, 52, 63, 65, 68, 72, 73, 75, 76, 85

Talisman   13, 49

Tao/Taoism (see Religion, *Dao*/Daoism)
Technology   86, 95, 97, 98, 99
   technocentrism   95
Temple   20, 25, 74, 78
Tiger (see Animal)
Tree   31, 38, 39, 47, 48, 49
   conifer   46–48
Trigram   3, 6, 8, 9, 10, 13, Fig. 3 (10)
   ba gua   6, 24, 49

Unity   5, 89, 95
Universe   29, 85, 89, 90, 95
Urban Redevelopment Authority (URA)   79, 80
Urns   1

Vegetation   16, 17, 87
Vital Energy (see *Qi*)

Wall   1, 31, 43, 45, 50, 51
Watercourses   4
Wealth   63, 96
White (see Colour)
White Tiger (see Animal)
Wind (see Element)
Wisdom   97
Wisma Atria   25, 52
Wu Xing (see Element)

Xue (see Cave)

Yang   8, 70, 107
Yellow (see Colour)
Yin   8, 16, 107
Yoon (Dr H. K.)   4, 16, 18, 20, 21

Zodiac (see Astrology)
Zuo shan xiang hai   14, 107

BRASH BOOKS BOOK CLUB
GRAHAM BRASH (PTE) LTD
HEAD OFFICE, SALES & WAREHOUSE
32 GUL DRIVE, SINGAPORE 2262.
TEL: 8611336, 8620437
TELEX: RS 23718 FEENIX GB
FAX: 65-8614815

We hope that you have enjoyed reading this book by **Graham Brash**. It is one in a list of over 600 publications covering a wide range of subject areas. To find out more about related titles, you can join our book club today.

BRASH BOOKS is a specialised book club which selects publications for its members according to their reading interests. Membership is free and book information, special discounts and other benefits (invitations to book-signings, for example) are mailed to members regularly.

To join **BRASH BOOKS**, simply complete this form and either fax or mail it to the above address. Upon receipt, a free catalogue will be forwarded to you. Thank you for becoming a **BRASH BOOK** reader.

Name: .... Tel/Fax: ....
Address: .... Date of Birth: ....
.... Occupation: ....
.... Marital Status: ....

Area(s) of Interest:

( ) Asian Interest   ( ) Others (please specify):
( ) Asian Literature   1) ....
( ) Mind, Body, Spirit   2) ....
( ) Business/Management/   3) ....
    Self-Improvement   Languages:
( ) Fiction – Adult   ( ) German
( ) Fiction – Children   ( ) French
( ) Education/Study   ( ) Others (please specify):
( ) General Interest   ....